How to Start a Training Program

Training is a Strategic Business Tool in Any Organization

Carolyn Nilson

Linking People, Learning & Performance

ASTD Press is an internationally renowned source of insightful and practical information on workplace learning and performance topics, including training basics, evaluation and return-on-investment (ROI), instructional systems development (ISD), e-learning, leadership, and career development.

Ordering information: Books published by ASTD Press can be purchased by visiting our website at store.astd.org or by calling 800.628.2783 or 703.683.8100.

Library of Congress Control Number: 99-72539

ISBN-10: 1-56286-118-2
ISBN-13: 978-1-56286-118-6

Table of Contents

Acknowledgments v

Chapter 1   Meeting the Challenge Head-On 1

Chapter 2   The Business Plan for Training 17

Chapter 3   Training Policy 29

Chapter 4   Training Standards 45

Chapter 5   Costs and Accountability 63

Chapter 6   The Business of Employee
             Development 97

Chapter 7   Introducing Training 125

Chapter 8   Analyzing Needs and
             Designing Training 145

Chapter 9   Delivery Options and
             Presentation Tips 173

Chapter 10   Performance and Evaluation 205

Bibliography 227

About the Author 231

Acknowledgments

Writing this book was fun. This is because in doing the field research for it, I had a chance to talk with a number of training practitioners—managers, coordinators, and specialists who are out there day after day figuring out how to get good training going in their companies.

Trainers in growing businesses are a creative and clever bunch. They have carried on the torch of learning at work, often in spite of being pulled in many directions other than training as their companies grow.

I would like to thank each of these persons whose interest and involvement in training in the growing business have given me valuable insights upon which to base this book. These companies and these people are:

Aetna Life & Casualty Insurance Company, Christopher Shafer, Design Consultant; **ARINC Companies,** Ursula Kuehn, Training and Communications Manager; **Becton-Dickinson,** Robert Stager, Technical Services Specialist; **Canyon Ranch,** Genevieve Driscoll, Human Resources Director; **Chamber of Commerce of Northwestern Connecticut,** Michael Witte-Meredith, President; **Cinderella Unlimited,** Morgan Finn, Owner, ICEO; **Geer Memorial Health Center,** Terrie Cawley, Inservice/Infection Control, and Jan Rathbun, Personnel Director; **Polytechnic University,** Brooklyn, New York, Dr. Charles W. Hoover Jr., Professor of IE/ME; **Howmet Corporation,** Jerome Rathbun, Manager of Human Resources; **IBM,** Tom Schappert, Manager of Management Development Programs; **InterActer,** Christian Nicolai, President; **Johnson & Johnson,** Robert P. Keigher, Director, Education and Development for Europe, Africa, and the Middle East, Charles Corace, Director Management Education and Development, and Linell Griffin and Evelyn Makkay, Administrative Assistants; **Millard Welding,** Jean Millard, Vice President; **Noack Organ Company,** Fritz Noack, President; **Northwestern Connecticut Community-Technical College (NCCC),** Jerome F. Rathbun, Tech Prep/Business & Industry Coordinator; **Patriot Properties, Inc.,** Richard C. Swadel, Executive Administrator, and Noel W. Nilson, Chairman, Board of Assessors, Town of Sandisfield; **Private Healthcare Systems Ltd.,** Margaret Sears, Corporate Trainer; **Quad/Graphics, Inc.,**

George Ryan, Director of Training; **SKF Specialty Bearings,** James Young, Human Resources Manager; **Sterling Engineering Corporation,** Joseph Lavieri, Chairman of the Board, John Lavieri, President, Roberta Moore, Quality Assurance Manager, and Patricia DiMartino, Personnel Administrator; **Stop & Shop Supermarket Winsted Store,** Charles Telford, Store Manager, Ed Wagner, Assistant Store Manager, Betty Begin, Customer Service Manager, Wally Beach, Stop & Shop Centralized Training Division Coordinator, and Terry Vandewater, Stop & Shop Director of Public Affairs; **The Torrington Company Standard Plant,** Joseph Harris, Training, Safety, and Employee Involvement Manager; **VSN-1 Personenvervoer,** The Netherlands, Hans Brouwer, Manager, Human Resources Development; **Wallace Company, Inc.,** Michael Spiess, Executive Vice President; and **Winsted Precision Ball,** Jeannine Frink, Personnel Manager.

I sincerely appreciate the time and talent of these caring and committed people in allowing me to interview them and to use their experiences as a foundation for this book. I thank each of them from the bottom of my heart for giving me permission to use their information and their companies' names in this book.

If I can translate the reality of their training challenges into practical help for others who are responsible for training in the growing business, then my goal will have been accomplished.

I am also deeply grateful to those who have assisted in the publication of this book. From the American Society for Training & Development (ASTD), I thank Nancy Olson, Vice President for Publications, for her leadership in securing resources and in moving the project along to timely completion; also ASTD staffers Mary Ann Armentano, Kathie St. Clair, Stacey Wagner, and Karen White. Also, I am grateful to our publisher colleagues who have granted permission to reprint their materials in this work: Irina Lumelsky, AMACOM Books/The American Management Association; Susan Sherman, Prentice Hall/Simon & Schuster; and Matthew Davis, the International Society for Performance Improvement (ISPI).

Chapter 1

Meeting the Challenge Head-On

Real people in real businesses struggle every day with making training "right" for the people who work in those businesses and for the company's bottom line. This introductory chapter snapshots some of these people and businesses as examples of excellence in approach to challenges common to many businesses committed to the power of workplace learning.

As a group, these companies introduce the critical variables of training for business growth. Later chapters deal with the variables in detail, providing practical guidelines and tools for cost-effective planning and delivery of good training within the special context of program startup.

Training and Mission

WALLACE COMPANY, INC., an industrial distribution firm in Texas, has a comprehensive quality mission statement that includes a section on training. It says, in part, that "training is integral to all areas of our operation and to all personnel." What's important about these good words is that with them the company gives validity and authority to the process of training as a critical contributor to the nuts-and-bolts functioning of business as well as to the human resources functioning of the work force. It's this dual capacity of training—to improve the work of business and to improve the workers—that this book is all about.

We begin with Wallace because of its size (about 280 employees), its deliberate decision to stay on top of change (shifting its market focus from engineering and construction to the less glamorous maintenance and repair), and its commitment to the people who make it work (going from a control mentality to a participation mentality with associates, suppliers, and customers). Emphasizing problem-solving teams of associates and comprehensive quality training, Wallace, in three years, increased its on-time deliveries 25 percent, its sales 69 percent, and its profit 700 percent. Wallace won the U.S. Department of Commerce Malcolm Baldrige National Quality Award in 1990.

In order to achieve this honor, Wallace, a family-owned business founded in 1942, essentially reinvented itself. Throughout this book, you'll see examples from the decisions and the results of the Wallace folks as they created new opportunities for their work force, their customers, and their bottom line. You'll see how Wallace put its commitment to training into action.

Through companies with a similar dedication to change, you'll see how training can be a needs-driven, customer-focused process tied to productivity and profit rather than the all too common unfocused, reactionary, hit-or-miss activity that it often is in the small and growing business. You'll see why we should stop saying "we're too busy to train." You'll see that training and the central mission of your business should be thought of together.

As a comparison as well as a contrast to the Wallace Company, we share with you the "Standards of Leadership" model developed recently by JOHNSON & JOHNSON (J&J). J&J is a multibillion-dollar, multinational megacorporation that specializes in the manufacturing and sale of a broad range of products in the health-care field. J&J's Director of Education and Development for Europe, Africa, and the Middle East forwarded to us the J&J "Credo Values" model used throughout the 170 J&J companies. As he says, "The only thing that hangs us together is our culture." You'll see how a company's view of itself can be communicated through training, and how J&J's leadership philosophy and practices can pervade a very decentralized operation. J&J shows the important linkage between training and corporate mission, and how the training operation functions as a strategic player in the company as a whole in all its diversity and throughout the world.

Commitment? Show Me!

BECTON-DICKINSON'S (B-D'S) Canaan plant is a several hundred employee medical device facility in Connecticut. Employees there work around the clock, with three shifts daily and two weekend shifts. They are part of the fast-growing health-care industry, providing disposable syringes and labware products to a variety of health-care deliverers.

The person in charge of training at B-D Canaan faces the major challenge of developing and delivering technical training for all

---

shifts equally, although, of course, he works only the first shift. As you read on, you'll see how organization, motivation, encouragement, and efficient training management allow him to accomplish his goals. This administrator of training has developed a way to turn people's commitment and involvement into action.

Flexibility and Focus

PRIVATE HEALTHCARE SYSTEMS, LTD. (PHCS) is a partnership of insurance companies formed for the purpose of creating programs to stem the rising cost of health care in the United States. It is headquartered in the Boston area, with offices in key U.S. cities across the country. It employs about 600 people nationwide.

Its employees typically work at computer terminals, with forms and data, and are involved in a large amount of customer contact by telephone. As Becton-Dickinson represents the supply side of the fast-moving health-care field, PHCS represents the data-intensive service side.

The PHCS work force typically has a hands-on understanding of clinical practice and includes many nurses. The staff is generally well educated. One of the challenges to the training manager is to maintain flexibility in scheduling to keep up with the company's rapid growth rate, projected at nearly 100 percent over the next few years. By being accessible and spontaneous, she has figured out a way to deliver good training in subjects somewhat "foreign" to her work force. She has learned to exemplify PHCS's slogan, "People Are Our Most Valuable Asset," by the way she has structured training services. In later chapters, you'll see how she has created a tight training system by focusing on flexibility and value for each training hour expended.

Performance

The SUPER STOP & SHOP SUPERMARKET in Winsted, Connecticut, is a growing business whose front line of customer service demonstrates the value of training oriented toward performance improvement. At Stop & Shop, as in some other supermarkets, adults with physical and mental disabilities perform jobs that require maximum interface with customers at the point of checkout and exit from the store. Customer service at a supermarket is a critical organizational function and a core process in a competitive business that depends heavily on satisfied customers. We spotlight this business as an example of training within a larger performance context, and show how a combination of centralized and on-the-job training worked to provide equal employment opportunity to employees covered under the Americans with Disabilities Act (ADA), as well as to support business growth.

Training for a Small World

SKF SPECIALTY BEARINGS COMPANY in Connecticut is part of SKF, a global company with sites in 70 countries. SKF is the world's largest producer of bearings. For example, it manufactures bearings that make dam gates work and enable tunnel boring machines to function. SKF Specialty Bearings Company is an example of a small business within a big business—a small, growing company with its own sales, financial, and human resources goals, yet with worldwide connections.

From a current 40 employees, the Connecticut plant had to gear up for an additional 40 workers, about half of whom came from Germany, to work on a new product. Training planners at SKF had to quickly institutionalize a bicultural training program appropriate for its size, its nonunion way of operating, and its business need to quickly be productive in spite of language differences. In later sections of the book, you'll see how other growing companies with an international profile are dealing with training their diverse work forces.

Extending the Family

STERLING ENGINEERING CORPORATION in Connecticut is a multigeneration, family-owned and -run engineering and machining company with strong ties to U.S. military and aerospace contracting. At its largest, it employed 230 people including quality control specialists, high-level machinists, and engineers. Brothers, sisters, cousins, and uncles head up key operations.

A job shop always under a time crunch, Sterling's big challenge is to be fast while incorporating the latest techniques in quality design, management, and control. In Sterling's lobby is a photo of two of its most prestigious products, the 15-pound backpack for NASA astronauts' space suits and its 6-pound spacesuit chest pack control unit. Sterling is often a custom technology subcontractor to large defense contractors such as Perkin-Elmer, Pratt & Whitney, and Hamilton Standard. In the president's office, an award for production excellence during World War II is proudly displayed.

Sterling's logo includes the words, "Machining and Tooling Excellence Since 1941." Promotional materials discuss its flawless performance and zero deviations. The quality assurance manager carefully describes the individualized quality training program of each engineer, and how she pays careful attention to providing the best possible training so that each person can continually contribute the best intelligence and skill to the job. The employee manual tells everyone that his or her responsibility during training is "to pay attention." Sterling has a history of placing a high value—and a high responsibility—on each of its trained shop employees. Training at Sterling Engineering has a highly individual feel.

Because it's small and family operated, yet tied to a vital industry, Sterling has the particular challenge of instilling the family's pride in the company and the family's sense of excellence in its next generation of managers, some of whom will probably not be members of the family. In order to do this, Sterling's leadership recently initiated a management development program for several nonfamily engineering graduates of Worcester Polytechnic Institute. Sterling made a commitment to an on-the-job management training program—just-in-time and just enough—to help extend its family.

Cross-Training as a Response to Turnover

The problems of both high turnover and low turnover are equally troublesome to trainers. CANYON RANCH, an Arizona-based complete health spa, is the kind of business that combines jobs whose turnover is low because of the personal nature of the work (such as fitness instruction and massage therapy) with others often associated with high turnover (such as dining room service). It is focused both on hospitality and hotel management and on individual fitness consultation and service. Canyon Ranch's Berkshire operation in Lenox, Massachusetts (about 400 employees), in addition, had recent start-up pressures that involved seeking large numbers of entry-level and part-time employees who needed to be trained to serve a wide variety of customers with a wide variety of services—and trained in a hurry.

One way that Canyon Ranch in the Berkshires dealt with the challenge of quality customer service in the face of a history of high turnover in the hotel business was to cross-train its employees. Department heads train their specialists to be competent generalists. That is, everyone knows how to handle the front desk, reservations, and guest services. Maintenance specialists learn how to back up the security force. Cross-training in this kind of growing business helps to assure quality in service and to present a united and caring front to guests who expect consistent and competent service. Cross-training is a way to provide a trained work force in all functions of your business in spite of turnover.

Team Training

Another example of cross-training is the kind of training that goes on among the team members of CINDERELLA UNLIMITED, a house-cleaning service headquartered in New Hartford, Connecticut. Cinderella Unlimited is a multi-person customized cleaning service that does business in 15 towns in northwestern Connecticut. It is the cleaning service that I use. Over the months of their working for me, I have observed the training practices of "the team" who work in my house. Like the spa and hotel Canyon Ranch, Cinderella Unlimited is a business historically characterized by high turnover. Like Canyon Ranch, it is to the great advantage of the business that service workers be cross-trained in each other's jobs. Unlike Canyon Ranch, Cinderella Unlimited makes a great point to the customer of working as a team.

Perhaps unique to itself, Cinderella Unlimited enjoys a very low turnover—in fact, half of the industry's average, less than one-third over the 20 years it has been in business. Cinderella's Owner/CEO, Morgan Finn, attributes this happy fact to team training and team work. Finn capitalizes on the natural inclination of people to work well together when they "like each other"; she pays particular attention to friendship and camaraderie, building teams from among individuals who like each other. She says "the team actually *holds* workers." This business has discovered the stabilizing effect of working in teams.

Cinderella's teams, however, are not always made up of the same people. For a host of reasons, such as reassignment for broadening or to fill in when someone is sick, a customer does not always see the same persons on the team from week to week. For example, my team is made up of four persons, some of whom are different from week to week. In order to assure consistent quality in the service it provides, Cinderella had to devise a training system to enable the "floater" team members to provide the same kind of customized services as the regulars, as well as all other floaters, and to provide services to the Cinderella Unlimited company standards.

At the start of our time together, I was asked to fill out a form indicating the special things about my cleaning problems and desires. My list included things like dust the leaves of the giant Yucca plant, be sure that the navy blue tile in the shower doesn't streak, don't put Windex on the acrylic picture frames but do put it on the glass ones, don't use chemicals on the piano keys, etc. The team leader for my job has this list with her. She tells the appropriate team member about these instructions and asks me to demonstrate or explain if necessary. I also fill out a checklist upon completion of my service to let Cinderella know "how the cleaning went today." On the feedback card there's space to comment on kitchen, bathrooms, vacuuming, dusting. There's also space for comments and compliments. Team members' names are on my card. This is a business that tries hard to make the customer part of the company's success.

When the team arrives in my house, in the context of the work to be done, the team leader makes task assignments and tells and shows team members, especially the floaters, what to do. When assigned tasks are done, team members help each other so that the work can be finished in a specified time period—in my case, four workers for one and a quarter hours. Teamwork and team training are essential to the commercial viability of this business, its competitive position in the field, and its longevity.

Focus on Training in a Stable Work Force

By contrast, many companies today have the opposite problem: low turnover because of a stable work force. This happens even in companies that are growing. A company vastly different from Canyon Ranch or Cinderella Unlimited, the WINSTED PRECISION BALL COMPANY in northwestern Connecticut, has the same challenge of providing customers with high quality capability in many areas of expertise.

However, Winsted Precision Ball's situation is that turnover has historically been low. People like to work there, and they tend to stay there. The company promotes from within, supports family life, and is proud of its presence in the community. Workers there number about 120, and, for nearly half a century, have made themselves a fine reputation for manufacturing miniature balls such as those used in ballpoint pens.

A new R&D facility opened in 1990 to explore new ball finishing processes and materials, taking the company solidly into the future. Its growth depends on both depth and breadth of knowledge and the skills of its stable work force. Winsted Precision Ball, which has considerable depth, cross-trains to ensure breadth in the face of low turnover. Employees learn their own production specialties well through formal apprenticeship training, but, in addition, are trained on the job to use a variety of inspection and high-tolerance machines. Weekly scheduled on-site management meetings, staff meetings three times per week, and bimonthly supervisory meetings off premises help to keep communication open, and function as forums for determining training needs.

Life After Safety Training

Many training managers in growing companies lament that safety training drives all training. The Occupational Safety and Health Administration's (OSHA's) recent muscle-flexing, environmental safety concerns, skyrocketing health costs for employers, and the population's general health consciousness have all created an expanded need for employee safety training in many companies. The American Society for Training & Development's (ASTD's) 1997 benchmarking study, for example, found that U.S. companies spent more money on safety training than on training for new employee orientation, sales and customer service, interpersonal communication, quality, and executive training (*Training Benchmarking Report*, p.3).

The typical pattern in many growing companies is for the production division to create a "safety coordinator" whose responsibility includes safety training. As business expands, the logical move often seems to be for that safety trainer to become responsible for all training.

This means that training is often placed in the operations side of the business, not the human resources side. This also means that production schedules, sales goals, and shipping timetables always take precedence over training schedules, sometimes having the effect of aborting well-planned training.

The burning issues for many safety trainers with added training responsibility are often when to seek a move into the human resources side of the business and how to create broad training opportunities for various kinds of employees.

The standard plant of THE TORRINGTON COMPANY, a division of worldwide Ingersoll Rand, with about 650 hourly and 150 salaried employees, is an example of a company whose safety manager also has training responsibility. His title is training, safety, and employee involvement manager. He is a 17-year veteran of the company, a manufacturing engineer, and an experienced production supervisor with demonstrated successes in working with manufacturing employees.

On his wall is a Total Quality Management training flowchart that reflects the company's commitment to ongoing training. He estimates that his safety responsibility accounts for half his time and includes monitoring tours of the factory, liaison work with the plant hospital, regular plantwide committee meetings, and other OSHA-mandated activities. Safety training programs include an accident prevention program, hearing loss prevention, back safety, hand-and-hand tool safety, respiratory training, and information on employees' right to know, the "hazardous communication" right that employees insist on these days.

He believes that his experience and personality will get him through the tough workload. He'd love to get career development programs for hourly workers started and would love to see more supervisory training of all sorts. He doesn't lack for ideas; what he'd really like is "a good man or woman Friday" to help with the execution of training—the development and maintenance of files, flip charts, manuals, and general training materials.

B-D Canaan's administrator of technical training also wears many hats—that of human resources representative, trainer of trainers, and safety program facilitator. He keeps himself organized by having two distinct workplaces within his office—two desks, two sets of files, two work tables, two bookshelves.

It's a sure bet that when safety training has been successful, employees see the need for and the benefits of other kinds of training. Good results are the best public relations for training. The safety trainer in the small and growing company has an unusually full job when other training responsibilities are added on. Life after safety training depends upon your strategic movement within the larger organization and upon the kinds of support you can create for yourself in order to accomplish broader training goals. And of course, good personal communications skills don't hurt either.

Computer Smarts and Customer Training

PATRIOT PROPERTIES, Inc. is a software-intensive, customer-focused service company with headquarters in Peabody, Massachusetts. Patriot Properties, Inc. produces professional appraisal software for municipalities to use in assessing their real estate and personal property in order to set their tax rates. Like many service companies, their success depends not only on the quality of the software product, but also on the ability of its customers to fully use the software. Customer training is a major, strategic core process of such a company. Training in this small company with big ideas is done online, through printed materials, by telephone help line, and in coaching and problem-solving one-on-one sessions in the context of the work to be done.

Patriot Properties started up in 1985 with a DOS-based assessing system, and converted later to the Windows-based system that it now uses, *AssessPro 4.0*. The company has about 40 employees and more than 100 customers, mostly towns and cities in Massachusetts, but including some municipalities in about a dozen other states. Theirs is a model of customer-centered learning that has kept Patriot Properties way ahead of its competition.

When Client Rights Are the Issue

GEER MEMORIAL HEALTH CENTER is a modern, comfortable long-term health-care facility, nestled on a New England hillside, whose 120 beds are mostly occupied by elderly residents requiring skilled nursing care. Approximately 175 employees work there, most of whom have the position of nursing assistant.

Like other small businesses with a strong commitment to human relations, Geer has a lower turnover rate than other similar facilities. Geer takes seriously its "Residents' Bill of Rights" and its "Open Door" policy. It goes beyond the legislated training and services required by the state Department of Health Services, the state Department on Aging, and the federal Ombudsman Reconciliation

Act (OBRA). Geer is generally one jump ahead of government-required paperwork.

Like safety coordinators, the person in charge of training in this kind of business is driven by federal and state training requirements dealing with personal safety and health. And like so many safety coordinators, she too wears many hats: fire and safety co-chair, infection control coordinator, employee health coordinator, intravenous committee chair, hospice committee member, and relief staff supervisor. Her title and her name badge say "Inservice/Infection Control."

Also like the expanded safety coordinator in other growing businesses, she doesn't lack for ideas. She combines a variety of media with on-the-job and classroom instruction to teach a wide variety of subjects way beyond those that are required. She says she'd be just fine if she could get rid of at least five other jobs.

Some of her biggest challenges are to keep Geer a premier place to work in the face of growth in the nursing care field. Competition for staff and differences in pay scales from region to region—and sometimes from town to town—posed by the home health aide movement keep entry-level training issues in the forefront. A management decision at Geer to open an Alzheimer's unit presents her with start-up as well as specialized training problems: Training in this case is an integral part of the business's marketing and long-term institutional survival strategy in a field where competition is heavy.

Unlike other types of businesses, the nursing care facility must operate under a Residents' Bill of Rights that guarantees clients comprehensive rights associated with self-determination, freedom of movement, and quality care. At Geer, there is an Open Door policy, which encourages residents to be a part of business meetings and business affairs of their choosing, so that they can understand and contribute to the normal business functioning of the institution. My own interview meeting was attended by a resident who could have been my mother. She came into our meeting through an open door, sat down, and participated in our discussion for as long as she chose to do so. And Geer's personnel director tells of her first day on the job when she was joined by three elderly gentlemen residents who wheeled themselves into her office to introduce themselves, to watch, and to assist her with her daily routines.

Obviously, this commitment to client rights presents special challenges to the manager of training. Not only does she need to be concerned with delivering the standard training in body mechanics, nutrition, anatomy and physiology, communication, spiritual care, and medications, but she must also train nursing assistants and other staff members how to *promote* and protect clients' rights. These are strong and contemporary challenges to trainers in the growing business of residential health care.

The Universal Cry for More and Better Management Training

Trainers in the trenches generally find a way to develop the job skills of workers who are responsible for new products, new machines, new processes, new systems, new procedures, new clients, and the day-to-day operations of business. Almost to a person, however, these trainers cry for managers and supervisors to get the same training as the operations folks. Many managers, too, say that they need more training.

QUAD/GRAPHICS, INC., a five-plant printing company headquartered in Wisconsin, found an inexpensive and highly effective way to train its managers to understand the jobs of workers. It taps managers to actually do the technical training and believes that "doing training is part of the manager's growth pattern." As Quad/Graphics, Inc.'s director of training says, "We arm-twist a little, but find that [managers] like to do the training." Quad has a big train-the-trainer program, having the spinoff of keeping the cost of training way down and creating a pretty solid emotional investment in the company at both worker and management levels. Using salaried employees in-house to do training also helped Quad cope with 50 percent growth per year during the last decade.

When managers talk about the training that they got or didn't get, they say things like: "I myself haven't had training since 1975"; "We don't have time for training"; "There's not much going on in management development"; "We sent a few [managers] out for seminars, but they weren't quite on target"; "Headquarters takes care of our management training"; and "We can't take our management or operations people off the job for training."

The personnel manager at HOWMET CORPORATION, a 250-person machining company in Connecticut, says that it is imperative that his work force have a better understanding of the company's military and commercial markets and a personal understanding of the basics of business financials—more specifically, costs, and how they impact individuals' specific jobs. Marketing and finance, two standard management training topics in this company, need to be funneled down to the work force. Whether it's funneled up or funneled down, management training apparently needs improving almost everywhere.

In terms of content, there seems to be a continuing need among supervisory and management staff for training in interpersonal communications, listening and giving useful feedback, conflict management and problem solving, how to provide career development for employees, time management, how to train employees on the job, updates on tax laws, and how to build quality into various business processes. Even in today's more sophisticated "involved" management, the business and financial basic skills must be taught as standards in the management training curriculum.

One Chamber of Commerce president tells of how member businesses regularly use the Chamber's conference room for company-sponsored training, often beginning at 7:30 a.m. and lasting for only a few hours. His estimate is that at about 300 employees, companies need a full-time training manager who can pay attention to both operations training and management training. And there seems to be a need for management training to be better coordinated, better planned, and more in synch with a company's current business operations.

Staying Ahead of the Competition

Within the reality of the cases above, and in the context of growing businesses everywhere, these are some of the key problems facing the growing business in the training arena and how some companies are beginning to solve them. Challenges and options for improvement surface as training problems and can be differentiated from interviewing problems, placement problems, job design problems, communication problems, and human resources general management problems.

Solving these training problems with some training system confidence and competence has helped growing companies like Wallace Company, Inc., Becton-Dickinson, Quad/Graphics, Inc., PHCS, Patriot Properties, and Stop & Shop Supermarket.

Similar challenges and options for improving training will be explored in the rest of this book. They are shared by those in growing companies of all sizes who have made a commitment to training and are ready to take the next step of doing it better.

Here are some challenges and options for improvement. In brief:

1. *Getting training tied to corporate strategy.* Write a business plan for training that meshes with the company's overall plan for growth.
2. *Preventing training from being "hit or miss."* Develop a training policy, communicate it broadly, and plan to carry it out.
3. *Making training concise and focused specifically on what you need.* Specify your own training standards.
4. *Figuring out the cost of training.* Create a realistic budget and identify who pays.
5. *Staying out of court and minimizing training paperwork.* Keep good records on training opportunity and job performance. Focus on competency and ability.
6. *Making it yourself or buying it outside.* Use a systems approach to training needs assessment. Be clear about what you need; don't be snowed by bells and whistles.
7. *Communicating about training.* Stay organized, offer variety, "polish your stars."
8. *Monitoring and evaluating training.* Determine process quality checkpoints. Involve a lot of people, including the trainees themselves. Give feedback for performance improvement.
9. *Developing careers through training.* Relate skill acquisition to improved performance, not necessarily to the annual salary review.
10. *Designing a high-quality course.* Build all courses on an instructional system design framework, regardless of course content.
11. *Tying training to the actual tasks of the job.* Before doing training, insist on a job analysis by some agreed-upon analysis method. Listen to employees.
12. *Delivering training that doesn't waste time.* Know the good and bad points about various ways to deliver training. Don't have tunnel vision in favor of the classroom.
13. *Making the most of computers and online services.* Invest wisely in hardware and software—and Web services—that will make your business run better. Look into renting or leasing, collaborative alliances with neighboring businesses or colleges, and bartering services. Hire computer-savvy teenagers or stay-at-home moms as temporary workers. Encourage online learning; take the time to train all employees in the skills *they* need for *your* business success.

14. *Making training "stick."* Know what you need to do to teach people and encourage them to learn, rather than just to give them an information dump.
15. *Breaking training down into pieces that can be learned.* Organize course content into units and modules that build on each other, being sure that each one is mastered before going on.
16. *Choosing the best training materials.* Go shopping with guidelines in hand. Keep focused on your objectives for learners. Choose or create materials with performance in mind.
17. *Training the trainer.* Learn about how adults learn, and be sure that your trainer does too. Design or buy a train-the-trainer course that takes into account learning styles, various kinds of motivation, how to give and receive feedback with adult students, and how to evaluate progress made by adult learners.
18. *Responding to a changing work force.* Analyze the real needs of your particular work force, keeping your eyes and ears open to the actual changes reflected in the makeup of your employee pool. Be creative in your design of training. Don't get carried away with media hype about training problems that might not appear among your own work force. Watch out for your biases, and be as honest as you can with yourself. Keep business goals in mind as you respond to a changing work force.

Hire smart, stay lean, listen to employees and customers, and think of training as both a management challenge and a design challenge. In the growing business, good training helps good people do a good job and goes right to the bottom line.

Chapter 2

The Business Plan for Training

Solid growth in training, like solid growth in the business as a whole, is the result—not the objective—of solid planning. The business plan for training gives the function of training the opportunity to be proactive, market-sensitive, and a visible contributor to corporate profits. It's the first document you, as the person in charge of training, should create as you begin to consider the value of the training operation to your company's overall business health.

Market Smarts and Training Planning

The training business plan is written in a persuasive way to indicate how training can be translated into profit. Like the corporate business plan, a training business plan examines the cost and pricing of the products or services it proposes. The writer of the training business plan, like the writer of the corporate business plan, focuses on the bottom line through careful market and financial analysis of the operation. The training business plan has the same profit goals as the corporate business plan, and the wise training manager will read the corporate business plan before writing a business plan for training.

Tying Training to Your Own Special Market

When you think in market terms about the viability of training, look for that special something that sets your business apart from the rest. First, focus on the market characteristics that give you an edge on the particular sales successes that you've had. Next, determine how you could plug training into your customers' potential training needs, as they relate to cost-effective use of what you sold them or to a value-added product or service from your "new look" employee training department. Reasons for writing a training business plan are found by looking both outward to customers and inward to employees.

Strategic Thinking

In the growing business, you have a golden opportunity to be a strategic thinker regarding human resources because small size and the momentum of growth generally speed up communication among all managers. The person in charge of training usually has quick and easy access to the CEO or company president. In short, if your antennas are up and working, you are probably aware of the management buzzwords and what business developments are generating the most excitement among top management. You have a chance to guide and lead your company forward through the vehicle of training *if* you're smart. Listen well around management staff meetings, and produce training planning documents that are tuned into mainstream management channels. As you figure out an angle for your training business plan, think about some of these questions:

- *Do you give faster turnaround on orders?* What very specific kinds of training do your employees need in order to maintain your commitments and levels of productivity? What dollar figures can you assign to a well-trained worker? How much does a well-trained employee save the company, compared to the average?

- *Is social or political change driving your success?* Have your company's profits escalated because of environmental awareness? Are you in the business of providing products or services for a niche in this kind of market? What do your employees need to know—and to internalize—regarding new federal, state, local, and industry standards that affect your operations? How can you go about finding out all the information they need in the fastest and most cost-effective way? How much will this investigation cost? How can good training optimize the transfer of information from rules and regulations to on-the-job savvy? Can you show that you've chosen the most efficient and effective training method?

- *Are you in the business because of proximity to a large corporation that needs what you can deliver?* Do you just happen to own and operate the warehouse across the field from the Japanese auto manufacturer's U.S. plant? What kinds of liaisons do you need in order to find out how to help your neighbor? Can these liaison persons be trained in how to look for training opportunities—what do your employees need in terms of knowledge and skills to serve the auto plant better? Are there special machines that you could lease or purchase to increase your business? What kind of training would your people need to operate these special machines? How much will it cost? How much additional business will a trained work force bring in?

- *Do you run your business for a niche market?* Fast Food Drive-Ins for Dieters has been your life. You are expanding the three hometown drive-ins to include 10 franchises throughout the states. Somewhere down the pike, probably within the next nine months, you'll need to train the franchisees in the procedures of the business. The counter people and food preparers will have to be trained in the methods of food preparation, storage, sanitation, safety, and a host of other skills that you have done by instinct as you've built the business. How much time can you devote to training? How much time do you have to spend writing training manuals? How much will it cost to get some consultant help to do this? What is the cost differential between your salary and the hourly rate you might be able to get a technical writer for? What is the typical cost of untrained labor? Should you hire only persons with experience in fast food drive-ins as a way to save training costs? What are the real savings either way? What are the incurred costs of failing inspections, litigation, defensive advertising? What are the dollar savings in time and trouble because you've had a good training program?

Whatever your company's special business focus is, tap into it as you create a business plan for training. Training will have an impact on your help-wanted advertising, on interviewing and hiring, on how fast your employees can produce good work, and on how long those employees will be happy and challenged working for you. The training business plan helps you codify and plan this critical business function.

Advantages of Writing a Training Business Plan

Here, then, in a succinct list, are the advantages of putting it down in writing. Think hard about all of the following before you are tempted to not go through the exercise of creating a training business plan—a discipline well worth the effort because it casts training as a vital contributor to the growth of the company.

- The market is analyzed to identify success factors and potential trouble spots.

- Customers are studied and perhaps contacted—more customer information never hurt anyone!
- If it's your own employees who need training, they are examined in terms of skill and knowledge deficiencies, giving you a better picture of the true targets that require training.
- Competing demands for funding are raised, forcing a prioritizing; in this proactive way, training at least has a chance of getting some funding.
- Change and growth in training operations are cast within the profit base of the company, tying training to other central business operations.
- Training is viewed as an initiating, vital corporate player instead of a peripheral operation always on the receiving end of whatever funds are left over.

Tools for Creating the Business Plan for Training

The six tools presented here take you step by step through the process of creating your own training business plan. Box 2-1 contains a brief summary of the six tools that are discussed in depth in this section. The guidelines, checklists, charts, procedures, and forms that follow were developed to take you right to the heart of potential problem areas in order to save you time as you set about writing your business plan.

Box 2-1. Tools for creating the training business plan.

1. *Format for a training business plan*—A quick outline of the key sections of the plan
2. *Content guidelines for each section of the training business plan*—A description of what to include in each section
3. *Steps in writing an executive summary*—A particularly important guide because often the executive summary is the only section that's read word for word—it has to be especially good
4. *Checklist of key points to cover in the rationale section*—Specific suggestions to help you avoid the typical pitfall of sounding too grandiose
5. *Models of training operational plans and timelines*—Examples of the three most commonly used operational plans and timelines: the standard timeline (sometimes called a Gantt chart), the PERT chart, and the flowchart
6. *Checklist for doing a business analysis*—A detailed checklist to be sure you've thought of everything when you do this important business analysis section of the document, which clinches the reasons why your proposed training deserves to be funded

---

1. Format for a Training Business Plan

Follow the format for a training business plan shown in Figure 2-1 to be sure you collect information in all the important areas before you actually write the document.

A Word to the Wise: Devote your best energies to the most crucial sections of the plan in the order of priority as found in Figure 2-1.

Figure 2-1. Training business plan format.

Executive summary
Rationale
Operational plan
Business and market analysis
Accountability and controls
Resource requirements

First priority: Business and market analysis
Second priority: Rationale
Third priority: Accountability and controls

The other sections will follow naturally if these sections are done well.

2. Content Guidelines for Each Section of the Training Business Plan

The following list describes the content you'll want to include in each section of your training business plan. The last two items, accountability and controls, and resource requirements, follow standard management fiscal control charts. These financial tools are considered in more detail in Chapter 5.

- *Executive Summary.* This section begins with a succinct summarizing statement defining exactly what is being proposed. This is followed by a brief description of each section of the business plan: rationale, operational plan, business and market analysis, accountability and controls, and resource requirements.
- *Rationale.* This section tells why you seek support for your program and how you project that it will be good for business in terms of dollars and cents.
- *Operational Plan.* This section contains a chart or timeline indicating the dates by which the operational decisions of

the proposed training program will be made. Add footnotes of clarification or explanation if necessary.

- *Business and Market Analysis.* This section is a judgmental and evaluative narrative based on hard data about the value to the company of your proposed training program. It includes discussion of market channels, market segmentation, probable clients or client types, identified competitors, projected sales, and projected profit figures. It also includes discussion of your training organization's strength in carrying out the program.
- *Accountability and Controls.* This section consists of a chart showing who is responsible for what action, how results will be measured, and by what date results are expected.
- *Resource Requirements.* This section estimates the dollar amount required by at least these four major resources: facilities, purchased services, equipment and materials, and staff.

3. Steps in Writing an Executive Summary

Take special care when you create the executive summary. Remember that it might be the only part of your plan that gets read by top management, so don't treat it as a simple summary. It is more than an outline because it is crafted for a specific group of your own executives. Follow these steps in order:

- Write to a specific executive or executives. Never begin writing until you know exactly for whom this plan is intended. Their names should be on the cover.
- Finish writing the plan.
- In your mind, summarize the material in the plan so that you can fit it on one or two pages.
- Begin the executive summary with a short introductory statement naming and describing the training program that you propose. Make this only one or two sentences.
- Review each section of the plan, rationale through resource requirements, extracting summarizing information.
- Put this summarizing information under headings that correspond to the five sections of the plan.

4. Checklist of Key Points to Cover in the Rationale Section

As you think about your rationale for proposing this particular training project, think always of the financial impact it will have on the business. Before you write anything, turn the financial impact around in your mind so that the outcome of your proposed training will be positive in terms of dollars and profit. Practice thinking positively, even if it means that it will take a year or so for the profit to be realized. Remember that a business plan is a document that justifies expenditure of resources in order to affect profitability. Here is a checklist covering the key points of the rationale:

Rationale Checklist

- ☐ The first sentence is short, a simple subject and predicate naming or defining the training project for which you seek money (**what**).
- ☐ The next two or three sentences briefly describe how the project will be carried out (**who, how, where, when**).
- ☐ The **why** section begins with a statement about why this training project will contribute to corporate profit. It includes a sentence that has a clause in it starting with "... because."
- ☐ The **why** section includes at least two more points regarding any of the following positives:
  - The advisability of acting now from an economic point of view
  - The savings to be realized at the conclusion of the project you propose
  - The cost-effectiveness of the staffing you propose
  - Savings down the pike because of the facility construction or consolidation that you propose
  - Projected profit because of getting a jump on the competition by acting now

5. Models of Training Operations Plans and Timelines

Here are several typical models for operational plans and timelines.
- *The Timeline.* Specifies decisions or tasks and the dates by which each should be accomplished, as shown in Figure 2-2(a).
- *The Program and Review Technique (PERT) Chart.* Features a network of decision points or operations. On the sample shown in Figure 2-2(b), the network of interconnected points is presented on a baseline of time so that each point clearly has a time target as well as a priority. Points on the left side of the chart must be completed before points on the right side of the chart, and all points interact with and affect all other points.

- *The Flowchart.* Describes processes, decision points, and results or products generally in a horizontal top-to-bottom fashion. A timeline can be run down the side to indicate the time frame in which each graphic in the flowchart should be implemented, as shown in Figure 2-2(c).

Figure 2-2. Sample charts and timelines.

(a) Timeline

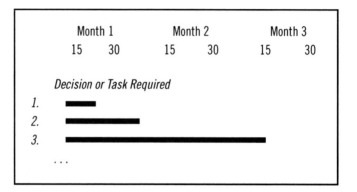

(b) PERT chart

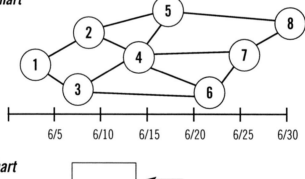

(c) Flowchart

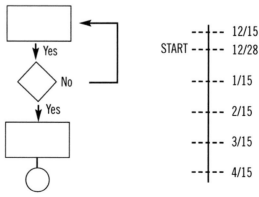

6. Checklist for Doing a Business and Market Analysis

Use this checklist to be sure you've touched all bases when doing a business and market analysis:

Business and Market Analysis Checklist

- ☐ Correct spelling and titles of informants and contacts
- ☐ Present competitors
- ☐ Future competitors
- ☐ Internal organizations competing for funding
- ☐ Track record of your own training organization
- ☐ Current capability of your training organization
- ☐ Projected growth phases of your proposed project
- ☐ Dollar effect on suppliers
- ☐ Probable sales volume
- ☐ Suggested margin rate
- ☐ Projected profit
- ☐ Customer needs
- ☐ Identification of market channels
- ☐ Approaches to customer groups

Typical Application of the Business Plan for Training

The following case study illustrates why a training business plan was needed and how the training manager of a growing company went about writing it. Notice how the person in charge of training saw an opportunity to expand customer service—and in a very profitable area—because of thinking strategically and backing up that strategic thinking with business planning.

Client Services in the Area of Facility Design

ENGINEERS ON CALL is a service company of 150 hardware and software engineers working on applications of electronic funds transfer. Its customers include brokerage houses, banks, and others in the financial services industry.

As part of its service, the company provides on-site training at the customer's location in the installation, maintenance, and operation of the funds transfer hardware that Engineers on Call designs. Often, the on-site engineers and customer trainers find that the customer's facility is poorly laid out and does not support training. Thus unnecessary manhours are spent in review and

Continued on page 26

Continued from page 25

troubleshooting, which results overall in driving up the cost to the customer during this transition period.

The manager of the customer trainers saw an opportunity to provide a formal facility design service to these brokerage houses and banks, for which the customer would pay a fee on a per diem scale. The focused and coordinated service that resulted saved the customer money in the long run and allowed Engineers on Call to broaden its services and make a good profit from a consulting service that cost the company virtually nothing. It also made training more effective because communications were clarified between the customer and the company's engineers and trainers. In this case, the payoff was in the ability of the customer training manager to think in terms of marketing an add-on training service—precisely the kind of positive business direction that a business plan so ably captures.

Focus on the Issues

- *Business Analysis.* The smart customer training manager saw an opportunity to add significant value to the services provided for the customer and to simultaneously contribute to the company's profit. An important issue here is the ability on the part of the customer training manager to see an opportunity to enhance the company's bottom line through better customer service.

The business plan for training included data about the problems that the engineers and trainers encountered, thus strengthening the case for initiating the proposed training facilities design service.

- *Communication.* This case also illustrates the importance of communication among the engineers who were sent out on installation and maintenance, the customer trainers, and the training manager. It's important in the small business to have a reporting structure, formal or informal, that facilitates communication. Especially in the small and growing business, better communication is often associated with training, so you'd better be ready to communicate effectively and cash in on its benefits.

Before writing the business plan for training, the customer training manager drew a flowchart of ideal communications and created some forms for recording observations and other operational data.

These were included in an appendix to the business plan. In the operational plan section of the business plan, she specified the reporting dates on which each of the forms would be used.

The Training Business Plan as a Vehicle for Bringing Training into Your Company

For the small or perhaps fragmented training department ready to grow, the training business plan is a good first step in institutionalizing training. It's a way for you to present training to top management so that they see its potential impact on results and profits. It's also a way for you to present yourself as a skilled leader, good corporate player, and strategic thinker.

In addition, the training business plan has a program or project focus. Often, this is exactly the sort of thing that top management needs in order to understand what the benefits of good training can be. Because it has parameters and controls, the risks of funding the training are clear. Because your business plan has data as well as projections, hard financials as well as analysis, it often can be the turning point for helping top management see what training can do for them.

Chapter 3

Training Policy

Training policy, like any other policy, is important because it states what you believe in. It provides a rallying focus and can act as a powerful motivator across departments within your company. Policy tells what you value; it helps to "center" the plans and actions of managers and employees alike. Policy keeps training on track so that it doesn't become a hit-or-miss event, and it motivates trainees to reach a little higher and stretch a little farther as they learn.

A training manager who publicly states a policy sends a signal that he or she is willing to act upon those statements of belief even when times get tough. Training policy delivers the message that training will be consistent and fair and that all trainees can be expected to learn under the same "rule of law."

What Drives the Creation of a Training Policy?

On a practical level, what drives policy formation has to do with products, sales, competitors, technology, customer service, margins, compliance and regulations, and overall good management. In addition, on the social and humanitarian level, companies often find policy drivers such as environmental concerns, being a good corporate citizen of your community, employee safety issues, hiring senior citizens, providing basic reading and math courses, and entering into job partnerships with public equal opportunity agencies.

Companies are often eager to get on the bandwagon of the latest industry focus such as "process quality," "supplier certification," "customer feedback," "zero defects," "cost-benefit analysis," "productivity," "performance," "employee decision making," and a host of other overarching directions that affect all the operations of the business. The trick for the training manager is to find out what these good words are in your company and then to translate these overarching ideas into the practical business applications that relate to sales, technology, production, good management, basic skills, safety, or whatever your pressing business needs are.

Making training policy is a strategist's job. To do it well means that you have to be where the good words are discussed and valued. It means that you can't hide behind course manuals, scheduling, needs assessments, feedback forms, and task analyses. It means that you have to get out of the narrow trainer's "busyness" and into management circles where corporate goals and directions are being discussed. You need to figure out how to do this if you're in charge of training, no matter what your title says and where you are positioned in the organization chart.

Translating Beliefs into Policies

In a technology company

In 1957, T. J. Watson of IBM said, "No matter how big we become, I want this company to be known as the company which has the greatest respect for the individual." This overarching human relations goal within the high technology business environment was the definer of IBM's unique "culture," and manifested itself over the years in three basic beliefs: respect for the individual, the best customer service in the world, and the pursuit of excellence in all that you do.

The practical business applications that followed from the "respect for the individual" belief included such commonly known policies as promotion from within, management development opportunities, and full employment. Training policies built upon these general policies included a full program of skill and career development courses to move people along to promotion opportunities, a wide variety of management development courses that focused on both breadth and depth, and training to maintain and enhance the stable work force to which IBM was committed.

In a financial services company

Posted liberally on corridors, on office walls, and in coffee cubicles throughout a city bank is a five-paragraph statement of human resources "values." The major focus of this single-page poster is the relationship between the bank's staff and its customers. This value statement is expressed in sentences that begin with "We will..." They include the following:

"We will know our customers' businesses."

"We will be proactive."

"We will be consultants and catalysts in dealing with our customers."

"We will be both responsive and responsible, knowledgeable, and discreet."

The training that was developed to reflect these values had to capture the essence of the bank's commitment: All employees would not only understand their own jobs but also "know the customer's business."

At this bank, these basic beliefs were translated into training policies and actions that helped all employees, from entry to executive level, to know the differences between public and privileged information in customer records, how to find and use a variety of information sources, and how to lead a customer into deeper understanding of the customer's own business. On a practical developmental level, this meant that some courses had to be rewritten to include data analysis skills or consulting skills. It meant that newly designed courses had to go through test runs with third-party evaluators to be sure that the courses in fact incorporated instructional strategies to accomplish the corporate goals.

In a consumer products company

A consumer products company was driven by customer complaints about slow delivery of products and services to become more responsive to its internal customers. This company developed a brochure outlining its mission, vision, objectives, and strategies. The essence of this document was a renewed pledge to customers that from this time forward, the company would do everything it could to make its business behavior economically viable, effective, and timely.

In terms of training policy, some of the strategies included: provide just-in-time training; meet regularly with customers to prioritize their needs; develop measures to analyze internal processes and teach employees how to use these measures; and establish training curricula to meet business needs of customers. Throughout the brochure, the "good words" all focused on delivering more timely and responsive training—and all sorts of other products and services that had a more direct, positive impact on customers' real business needs.

In a distribution company

In WALLACE COMPANY, INC., the 1990 small-business winner of the Malcolm Baldrige National Quality Award, training policy was developed around the "quality" goals that drove the company's actions as it organized itself to compete for the award. In the human resources arena, Wallace set the ambitious goal of 100 percent staff participation in quality training—training in the measurements and monitoring systems that were related to each person's job. Wallace, a company of 280 people, spent about $700,000 in three years on training.

In its Quality Mission Statement, Wallace says, "We are committed to the precepts of Continuous Quality Improvement, Customer-Driven Service, Product Quality, Statistical Process Control, and Employee Involvement." As an industrial distribution firm, Wallace astutely realized that its vendor and supplier quality standards had a direct impact on its own quality. With an eye to its ultimate customer—and the link between the supplier, itself, and the customer—Wallace embarked on an ambitious vendor certification program. It became the first company in its industry to initiate a supplier training program in Continuous Quality Improvement, molding key suppliers into a quality conduit that yielded dramatic results. Training's statement of "commitment" within the Quality Mission Statement says that "training is integral to all areas of our operation and to all personnel." The results—a 700-percent increase in operating profits in three years and the Malcolm Baldrige National Quality Award—bear witness to the effectiveness of the training policy that provided quality training to every person in every operation of the business.

Essential Elements of Training Policy

When you get to the point of putting your beliefs and commitments on paper—that is, of writing your training policy—be guided by this simple format:

First, the **value** statement
Second, the **belief** statement
Third, the **action** statement

Here are some examples of training policy statements at two companies.

A residential health center

The **value** statement: It is the mission of this Center to promote and protect residents' rights and help residents to exercise them.

The **belief** statement:	We believe that individual dignity is essential to a healthy life, and that working together through information, training, and personal assistance, we will all be better citizens of this residential community.
The **action** statement:	Therefore, the Training and Development Department will (1) coordinate training efforts with the Client Information Office so that the medical and social services staff receives timely training related to scientific and regulatory information, (2) seek out and provide training in the latest nursing care techniques, emphasizing both breadth and depth of skill and knowledge, (3) commit training funds to purchase a set of videotapes on models and challenges of personal assistance, and (4) develop a Centerwide personal assistance training program emphasizing role play, simulations, and hands-on microtraining.

An R&D systems development laboratory

The **value** statement:	We will live by the values of integrity, innovation, and collegiality.
The **belief** statement:	We believe that all employees are peers in this endeavor, driven by the relentless pursuit of design excellence.
The **action** statement:	We will provide a broad range of training programs with the aim of assisting employees in increasing their depth and breadth of knowledge in their specific narrow disciplines. Because training is essential to this company's leading edge, training is positioned as a cost center or staff service, equally and openly available to any employee who needs training to enhance the job. A minimum of 30 hours of training per year is recommended for all design staff. Design associates have the choice of such training options as internal rotations, university short programs, technical skills seminars, monitored mentoring, and facilitated brainstorming groups.

Enhancing the Basic Training Policy Statement

There are two additions to the basic value-belief-action formula for writing policy that can sometimes clarify and direct your policy into more immediate action. These are (1) a section of *challenge* to employees as they begin operating under this policy and (2) a section listing the company's or department's *responsibilities* to the trainee so that vision or values can, in fact, be acted upon through training. These responsibility areas include such things as relaxing productivity quotas during training times, allocating corporate funds to equitably finance training across organizations, keeping good records, and providing incentives and recognition for training accomplishments.

Advantages of Writing Down Training Policy

Policy is the operational framework that provides guidance for action. It is an expression of your beliefs and intentions, and is tied, therefore, to the culture you have or hope to create. Your taking the time to think in terms of training policy will help all those around you see the possibilities that training has for making the business better. These are the advantages of having a written training policy:

- You've connected your operational goals and plans to the value system of the company.
- You've recognized that stating what you believe in is a powerful focus for ensuing action.
- You've demonstrated that training intends to be an important contributor to furthering the corporate culture.
- You've shown that you understand how training can be a member of the corporate team.
- You have a piece of paper that can be sent around to all employees so that everyone gets the same message and there's no doubt about what you mean.

An Example from Johnson & Johnson

JOHNSON & JOHNSON, known to most of us as the Band-Aid company whose many products fill our medicine cabinets, has another perspective on training policy. At J&J, all policy emanates from J&J's corporate "Standards of Leadership," which are centered on the company's "Credo Values." That is, corporate policy comes first;

training policy in fact is corporate policy, and it all is grounded in the Standards of Leadership.

J&J's Director of Education & Development for Europe, Africa, and the Middle East, Robert P. Keigher, a member of ASTD's Benchmarking Forum, talked recently about the J&J approach. He makes the point that a company's "culture"—its approach to problem solving, its norms of behavior, its sense of shared values—is the only thing that holds a company together in the long term, no matter what the size of the company. At J&J, that company culture is defined by its Standards of Leadership document, which had its origin in Chairman and CEO Ralph S. Larsen and Vice President of Education and Development Allen Anderson. Through a series of task forces at line manager level, top management sought and received input from a wide base of "local" leaders who helped to define exactly what J&J leadership is. What resulted was the Standards of Leadership document, a reference guide featuring a pinwheel-like graphic on its cover, and inside, a listing of standards of behavior expected of J&J leaders at all levels of influence in the company. The Johnson & Johnson pinwheel is reproduced, with permission, in Figure 3-1.

Figure 3-1. Standards of Leadership: Johnson & Johnson.

The five blades of the pinwheel are Customer/Marketplace Focus, Innovation, Interdependent Partnering, Masters Complexity, and Organizational and People Development. All spin out from the Credo Values and Business Results at the center of the model.

Inside the reference guide, the six major components of the pinwheel are elaborated with bullet lists specifying the action or behavior that should be demonstrated in order to meet the standards of leadership, no matter what job a person holds. One is struck immediately by the very practical action focus spelled out in this document. For example, the six bullet items in the Credo Values part of the model say:

- Behaves with honesty and integrity
- Treats others with dignity and respect
- Applies Credo values
- Uses Credo Survey results to improve the business
- Balances the interests of all constituents
- Manages for the long-term

Business Results include:

- Cash flow
- Cost effectiveness
- Customer satisfaction
- Environmental/safety responsibility
- Income growth
- Market share
- New product flow
- People development
- Product quality
- Productivity
- Regulatory compliance
- Volume growth

Throughout the document, the message comes through that J&J people have a vision of the future across many boundaries, listen to customers, leverage their products and services, not only master complexity but know how to manage it, and are expected to create an environment of achievement for optimal performance.

All of this adds up to a pretty powerful elaboration of the mission of a corporation, as seen in the model for leadership encouraged in all employees. Bob Keigher's operation, Education & Development, uses the model as the major focus of a four-day leadership workshop that is run around the world. It is used during succession planning, is its own Web site on the corporate intranet, and has been incorporated into J&J's performance management system. It is an example of how corporate policy goes laser-like throughout a corporation, facilitated in large part by its education and development mandate.

Tools for Writing Your Training Policy

The three tools presented here lead you into writing your training policy. Box 3-1 contains a brief summary of the three tools discussed in depth in this section. The guidelines, checklists, charts, procedures, and forms have been created to spark your imagination about where to find the best reasons for policy creation in your company. They recognize the reality that you're probably new to the idea of training policy, whether you've been on the job for a while or you're new at the job of running the training operation. These three tools take the mystery out of what might seem like a frightening and obscure exercise.

Box 3-1. Tools to help you write your training policy.

1. *Checklist of areas where training policy can be useful*—A very specific list of the best places to find reasons for creating a training policy
2. *Training policy template*—A graphic pattern of what goes into a training policy statement, followed by an expanded outline chock-full of specific examples of the exact words to use
3. *10 ways to put training policy into action*—A guide to actions that you can take to be sure that your policy development efforts pay off

---

1. Checklist of Areas Where Training Policy Can Be Useful

If you are just beginning to get your training organization together, or you'd like to gain more visibility for the training that you already do, the following checklist will help you to decide where to look for training policy opportunities.

Remember that training policies can be written to cover large topics such as productivity and quality, or they can be written to focus on small topics such as English as a second language for a target group of employees.

Use the checklist as a guide to options through which training policy can lead to a stronger work force. Develop training policy in any of the areas listed.

Areas for Training Policy

☐ *Employee safety:* lifting, chemical hazards, respiratory hazards, VDT glare and radiation, carpal tunnel syndrome, hearing, sight, lighting, noise

☐ *New skills:* computer systems and software, new machines, new sales strategies, new accounting approaches, new design approaches, new algorithms, new technical writing styles

---

- [ ] *Equal opportunity:* career development for minority workers, remedial math or writing for employees at the low end of the literacy continuum, English as a second language for foreign-born workers, skill development for older workers, reorientation training for part-time workers, initial orientation to company and to department or organization
- [ ] *Customer service:* attitude development; your messages through body language, voice, and eye contact; active listening; customer needs analysis; two-way communications; complaints; repeat business
- [ ] *Productivity:* solving people problems, troubleshooting machinery, statistical process control, making work teams work, documentation and reports, self-monitoring techniques, just-in-time techniques
- [ ] *Communications:* procedures, information sources, benefits and personnel matters, standards, clarification of roles (supervisor, manager, employee)

2. Training Policy Template

Use the template shown in Figure 3-2 to draft your own training policy statement. Follow any of the options presented.

Figure 3-2. Template to follow when drafting training policy.

The **value** statement
The **belief** statement
The **action** statement
Challenge to employees *(optional)*
Company's responsibility *(optional)*

3. Expanded Example of the Training Policy Template

The following list of items shows how the basic training policy statement can be worded in different ways. You'll note that each basic part of the statement (value, belief, action) has three different options for expressing that part. Choose any of these, or develop your own way of saying it.

The **value** statement:	1. It is our mission to ....
	2. This company's overarching goal is to ...; therefore, the training organization will strive to ....
	3. We value the qualities of ....
The **belief** statement:	1. We believe that employees deserve ....
	2. Our belief in ... drives our commitment to ....
	3. No matter how big we grow, we will hold fast to our historic working philosophy that ....
The **action** statement:	1. In order to accomplish our goals, training will take the following actions: (a) ... (b) ... (c) ... (d) ....
	2. Therefore, the Training and Development organization will initiate a program of ...
	3. Because of our strong commitment to human resources development in this company, we will assist each employee in developing, monitoring, and evaluating an individual training program, beginning on January 1, 2001.

[Optional statements]

The **challenge** statement:	1. We challenge each employee to develop and maintain a training opportunity plan and to review it quarterly with the training specialist and the employee's supervisor.
	2. To ensure swift operational results from training, we challenge each employee to review training materials two weeks after training has finished, to post the skills list in a convenient place near his or her PC, and to attach the instructional hot line phone number to the front of his or her telephone.
The **responsibility** statement:	1. In order to recognize increased competence through training, the company will semiannually sponsor a "Competency Award" ceremony at which bonus points will be awarded.

These points are exchangeable for dinners out, half-days off, spa weekends, and tennis or golf days.

2. We guarantee a safe work environment for each employee. After training, each employee will receive a personal VCR and safety videotape reinforcing safe procedures and detailing the report chain in case of safety deviations.

4. Ten Ways to Put Training Policy Into Action

Here are some specific actions you can take to reinforce your policy development efforts:

1. Talk about your policy at orientation of new employees.
2. Give copies of your statement to recruiters and personnel representatives.
3. Ask your personnel staff to discuss training policy at the same time as they discuss benefits, especially at the time of hiring.
4. Ask supervisors to make training policy review a regular part of the annual performance discussion with employees. Encourage employees to make training plans with the agreement of their supervisors.
5. Post the policy liberally throughout offices and shops, especially where groups of employees tend to gather.
6. Periodically mail a copy to each employee.
7. Include a copy with the information packet that is given to each trainee in each course that you sponsor.
8. Get yourself invited to executive meetings so that you can explain the policy and report on progress.
9. Make a promotional videotape about the training policy and show it once a month in the employee cafeteria.
10. Write newsletter or newspaper articles about successful training to show how policy is implemented throughout the company. Be sure to include photos in your article.

Typical Application of Training Policy

The following case study illustrates why the central training group at Suburban Bank decided to develop a training policy and how it looked on paper.

Developing a Training Policy

SUBURBAN BANK'S headquarters is located in a small city. At this location, a central training organization, triggered by a new vice president and one new instructional technologist, decided to revamp itself. Like banks everywhere, Suburban Bank seemed to be jumping through hoops in constant reaction to what appeared to be the "new product of the week," new regulations, new boxes on the organization chart, and an economy that alternately slumped and raced ahead. Competition in banking was fierce, and business as usual was beginning to look like a game of survival of the fittest.

Obviously, to deal with this kind of change in an industry where change had become the constant, banks had to employ a well-tuned, astutely aware, knowledgeable, and skilled work force. The problem that Suburban, like so many other banks, faced was that most of the management employees had joined the bank at a more placid time when banking attracted conservative folks who appreciated stability and tradition. Training's challenge was to bring the employee resource pool up-to-date in its knowledge base, its skills, and its attitudes toward the business it now found itself in.

Developing a written training policy was an especially effective way to reach the management staff. Writing it down appealed to the managers' sense of orderliness and good planning. The training policy, in brief, had these components:

The **value** statement: Suburban Bank believes in providing our customers with cost-effective, value-added products and services. All that we do is driven by business needs.

The **belief** statement: In order to fulfill this corporate mission, the Central Training Group begins with the conviction that we must be proactive in human resources strategies, taking the initiative to add, delete, and modify programs; and that we must find ways to codify and evaluate performance, figuring out cost-effective solutions to performance problems. We believe that training can be tied to Suburban's business goals and plans.

Continued on page 42

Continued from page 41

The **action** statement: In order to serve our customers with competitive banking products and services, we will train and retrain our staff:

- Through a training system that is tied to unit business plans at the needs assessment phase
- By training budget development tied to specific department objectives
- Through increased financial monitoring regarding return-on-investment of training development and delivery dollars
- By revising curriculum to reflect topics of current strategic relevance only
- By determining the most cost-effective training delivery methods, making the best use of new electronic and video systems
- By offering all employees a dual track of professional development training opportunities—a skills-based track featuring new courses in automation, performance systems, and computerized strategic planning; and an applied management track featuring new courses in legal and regulatory innovation, trends in world banking, and new approaches to developing staff

Focus on the Issues

The preceding case study illustrates how a growing bank used the creation of a training policy statement to position itself in a proactive leadership position within itself as it went through major changes. The two issues, immediacy and change, were addressed by this training policy.

1. *Immediacy.* An important issue in this policy development case is the desire of the policy writers to make a statement that is immediately reflective of the turbulent times. This is a training policy that is narrow in focus. Its intent is to propel the new training management staff into action on the immediate issues of the business.

2. *Change.* Another important issue in this policy is its narrow focus on change. Those who read the training policy will get the message, through the action statements, that change is about to happen. This is especially apparent in the action statements, each of which commits the training group to a different way of doing some function of training. In this brief policy, the training department positioned itself to be a leader of the changes the bank was currently experiencing.

Training Policy as a Way to Keep on Track

The use of a training policy will help the training organization that has a nucleus of people ready to go to work building a strong strategic department coalesce as a work group. It will help you keep your in-house development and revision work on track, and it will keep you focused on your own goals as you deal with vendors and consultants. It will help you talk intelligently—with corporate goals in mind—as you deal with upper management and customers. A training policy can set both you and the company's employees straight as funds are allocated for training. And it can help you raise your sights as you get bogged down in daily problems of scheduling, expenditure of resources, and tight development timetables. In short, a training policy motivates through belief and commitment—two powerful organizers of the best resource you have, your human resources.

Chapter 4

Training Standards

Standards provide the rules under which orderly work progresses. It's especially important for training work to operate under strict rules because training is particularly susceptible to being a disorganized, an unplanned, and an inconsistent business function.

Training standards should define the measurements that tell employees what's expected of them in terms of performance. They often contain reference points regarding human resources quality and productivity. Training standards provide the rules for the products associated with training (the evaluation forms, audiovisual materials, training manuals, course objectives, classroom exercises, and instructional software), as well as for the processes that people engage in as training is being developed and delivered.

Why Bother with Training Standards?

CEOs Are Disillusioned

During a regional conference of ASTD in Newport, Rhode Island, a national study was discussed by the conference's keynote speaker. This was a study of a large number of CEOs who attempted to define their burning management issues for the immediate years ahead.

What emerged from the study was that operating strategies, not the traditional financial strategies, were the biggest challenges. A whopping 83 percent of these CEOs stated that human resources was their first priority—well above international issues, information technology, and capital and financial issues (each averaging about 25 percent of the vote). Human resources concerns were followed by a very high 70-percent vote for strategic planning issues as the next most pressing challenge for the CEO.

Further analysis of the human resources issue revealed that these CEOs lacked confidence in the quality of human resources advice, felt uncomfortable with the way their human resources staff resolved problems, said that their human resources organizations had few comprehensive strategies, and therefore they (the CEOs) were unwilling to commit capital to the human resources organization.

These are pretty strong words, implicating training in places where it is a part of the human resources organization and raising the red flag of challenge in places where training is outside of the human resources organization. In either situation, the message is clear—in order for training to be a viable business function, and it obviously needs to be, it must get its act together in terms of planning, managing, communicating, and measuring. Efficient and successful operations depend directly on a strong and well-tuned work force.

A Coherent System Improves Performance

ASTD's Laurie J. Bassi and Mark E. Van Buren have done the training community a great service during the past few years by conducting and reporting on their benchmarking studies, in which they show what the outstanding training departments are doing. Data from more than 800 organizations was presented in the study conducted in 1998, featured as "The 1999 State of the Industry Report" in the January 1999 issue of *Training & Development* magazine.

Among the interpretive commentary is this observation at the beginning of the report: "Our analyses indicate that, over time, training investments—especially when situated within a coherent system of human performance practices—are clearly associated with improved firm performance." An interesting bit of advice from Bassi and Van Buren for those trainers interested in approximating leading-edge practices is to first envision the system: "A good starting place for your leading-edge makeover isn't how much you spend on training, but rather the things you do to improve workplace learning and performance in general." A *coherent system* is the operative phrase. Setting training standards and working to meet or exceed them can be a foundation for system coherence regarding individual performance and workplace learning.

A brochure from The Conference Board in New York recently found its way to my mailbox. It advertised "The 1999 Strategic Learning Conference: A Tool Kit to Power Business Performance." The conference is pitched as the "first-ever" conference to facilitate learning how to measure and assess strategic learning, among other things. The point is clear: Business strategy in the form of strategic learning can translate into organizational change and competitive advantage. Training standards need to be a part of the same kind of thinking as "strategic learning." System coherence is the goal of strategic learning.

Human Capital Is Seen as America's Hope

Robert Reich, one of the foremost economists in the United States and Secretary of Labor in the first Clinton administration, wrote in the February 1991 issue of *The Atlantic Monthly* that the success of American capitalism no longer depends on the private investments of highly motivated capitalists, but rather on the unique attributes of our work force—the accrued skills and insights of American workers. He points out that historical types of capital no longer have a single nation's identification. Today, loans, shares of stock, factories, offices, and research labs move around the world "with scant respect for national boundaries."

Reich concludes that because the traditional capital structures of business are truly worldwide, what identifies a nation's economic strength now is its "educated brainpower." He suggests that in the search for profitable national commodities, the only value that cannot be easily replicated worldwide is the value found in a nation's specialized problem-solving and brokering services such as research, engineering, design, marketing, consulting, and other high-level types of management skills. Matching ideas to particular markets is what will pay off in terms of cashing in on America's wealth. Reich's ideas nearly a decade ago became part of a foundation of economic thinking that led to our current broadened view and operationalizing of intellectual capital and knowledge management systems.

Training Is a Way to Add Value

On a practical level, those in charge of training must find ways to capture the processes by which people at work increase their skills and deepen their insights. Trainers must develop monitoring and measuring systems that motivate employees to learn more and better; trainers must create training courses, conferences, manuals, videos, and one-to-one learning situations that are geared to efficient and purposeful learning results. Especially in the growing business, trainers have a wonderful opportunity to "push" the direction of growth through training policy and standards.

Trainers can look for performance indicators in many kinds of operations documentation and see why they should "bother" developing training standards. For example, quality assurance studies can point out what products, processes, and employees could benefit from training and at what level. Specific products, customers, and organizations can be targeted for specific kinds of training, making training a part of business solutions. Reports of on-the-job injuries can directly point to the creation of safety training standards, having an impact on insurance costs, absentee rates, and productivity. Marketing plans and strategic plans can target the need for better customer service training, sales training, and management training. New systems and equipment, or pending orders for other capital items, can drive the creation of training. R&D operations can require new kinds of design, theoretical, and statistical training.

In any company, there are numerous places to look for opportunities to create training standards. The secret is to believe in training as a central business function, capable of making a huge difference in the value of the company's people asset. The concept of human capital as an enormous source of economic strength requires a foundation of policy, strategy, planning, and standards to support it. This is why you bother with training standards.

Typical Components of Training Standards

Standards are measurement specifics. They typically tell what's expected in terms of numbers, frequencies, percentages, or some amount of approximation toward a measurable goal. Standards focus on the probably attainable ideal—on the expected outcome.

Standards are usually categorized or grouped in logical units. They relate to policies and business planning statements. They generally are stated using some of the same "good words" as are found in policy statements and business plans. They tie directly to the current management directions of the company.

Training standards should have an apparent relationship to both the processes and the products of a company. For example, training standards should reflect the company's information and communications management; sales and customer service, production, career development, and overall human resources management; financial and accountability processes; quality assurance processes; and processes such as leading and supervising. Training standards should also focus on the tangible items associated with the training organization itself—such as instructor manuals, trainee manuals, graphics materials and equipment (overhead transparencies and slides), job aids, training conferences and field trips, training videotapes and films, distance learning protocols, online and computer-based training (CBT), and parts of courses such as outlines and units, lists of objectives, practice exercises, glossaries, course handouts, and evaluation forms.

Training standards can be developed around the business of training—standards for who should be trained and how much training certain categories of employees should receive; standards for balance between new courses created and old courses revised; standards for penetration into internal departments that may not have used training services in the past; standards for marketing training to suppliers or customers; standards for working with vendors and consultants as they develop or deliver training for you; standards for pilot testing a new course; and standards for training's contribution to the company's profit.

Advantages of Having Training Standards

These are the reasons why developing training standards is worth the trouble:

- Everyone who's involved with training development and delivery has the same rules to follow.
- Even people without a training background can often help develop or deliver training if standards are clearly written and attainable.
- People who operate under standards know where they stand. They can monitor themselves and receive objective feedback if they're unable to attain the set standard. With standards, there's little room for misinterpretation.
- Standards help get an inexperienced training staff to work toward common outcomes.
- Standards can save you time in training your trainers.
- Standards let others know that you understand your business of training in all of its many aspects.
- Standards promote consistency and reliability.
- Standards help guarantee equal opportunity under the law.
- Standards promote correctness, accuracy, completeness, and validity.
- What gets measured usually gets done.

Tools for Creating Training Standards

Three tools with extensive examples are included here to show you exactly what standards are and how you can copy the ideas in your own company. The tools, which are summarized in Box 4-1, are meant to suggest specific places where training standards can be developed—in the most common areas of responsibility: delivering a range of courses, running the training operation, and creating all the internal parts of a specific course. The matrix, samples, and layout were developed for you because standards can be a tricky item—the secret to creating useful standards that work for you is to think in terms of what can be measured or counted.

Box 4-1. Tools to help create training standards.

1. *Training Standards Development Matrix*—A comprehensive matrix of 15 cells highlighting the key measurable items in five of the most common types of training and several pages of expanded examples of selected items from the various cells in the matrix

2. *Samples of standards for administration of training*—A targeted set of samples tied to upper-management goals, "process" quality, and the nuts-and-bolts administrative functions of running the training operation

3. *Layout of a standards document for development of a new course*—A "quality" list of both the processes and the products of course development that any new course must go through, a guide for measuring the design process

---

1. Training Standards Development Matrix

The matrix in Figure 4-1 points you to places to look when you want to create training standards. No matter what kind of training you do—from customer service to management training—you'll find things that can be measured. This matrix suggests work processes, business results, and characteristics of individual productivity that can and should have standards developed around them. Use the matrix to spark your imagination regarding places to look when creating training standards. Add your own items to cells in the matrix. When you design training, build training standards into your training and focus on what can be measured; then set your sights high.

Figure 4-1. Training standards development matrix.

Training	A *Work Processes*	B *Business Results*	C *Individual Productivity*
1 Customer Service	**A1** • Communicating image • Identifying/verifying needs • Providing what customers need • Cultivating repeat business • Supportive systems and procedures	**B1** • Orderly and timely service • Number and nature of complaints • Repeat business	**C1** • Time to satisfy the customer • Completeness of service • Documentation and accountability • Follow-up and feedback
2 Production	**A2** • Planning and forecasting • R&D • Quality assurance • Engineering/design • Communication • Testing • Inventory control	**B2** • Errors/defects • Rejects • Deviations • Quantity shipped • Inventory	**C2** • SPC • Pieces of output • Timing • Cost per unit • Accident rate
3 Sales	**A3** • Applying sales techniques • Knowing product features/benefits • Managing time • Listening to prospects • Problem solving • Closing sales	**B3** • Qualified prospects • Cost containment • Time expended • Variety of sales • Number of sales • Profit	**C3** • Time/cost per sale • Profit per unit • Rejections • Customers • Commissions

Continued on page 52

Continued from page 51

4 Systems	A4 • Operating systems • Data communications and networks • Hardware function • Software design, development, and evaluation • Programming • Support systems	B4 • Downtime • Bugs • Lines of code • Service calls • Hot-line responses • Documentation clarity	C4 • Time on task • Processing time used • Development errors per line of code • Reliability • Accuracy • Revisions • Rate of problems solved
5 Management	A5 • Managing work flow • Solving people problems • Managing benefits • Dealing with unions • Accounting and budgeting • Accountability • Planning • Assuring safety • Interviewing and hiring	B5 • Deliverables • Schedules • Absentees and lates • Overtime and temporary help • Contracts • Grievances • Profit • Accidents • Turnover • Satisfied customers	C5 • Deadlines met • Quotas delivered • Work force stability numbers • Margin and profit • Overhead containment • Accuracy of business projections • New hires retained

Work processes

The following group of examples shows, through simple models, how to create training standards in typical business operations. These examples of training standards are based on selected items in the training standards development matrix shown in Figure 4-1. Each example includes a reference to its cell location.

Customer service training (example from cell A1)

The standard of listening to customers: All courses will be rewritten during July and August to include a unit on needs identification and verification. The style of each new section will feature step-by-step procedures and how-to text so that customer service representatives can quickly and effectively use on the job what they learned during training.

The standard of adequate training for support staff: Each customer service representative is responsible for identifying two support staff members who could benefit from training in systems and procedures during the next fiscal quarter.

Production training (example from cell A2)

The standard of relevant management training: Production managers will take three out of five courses in the Planning and Forecasting curriculum within one year of their promotion to the manager position.

The standard of engineering excellence: The Technical Training Department will provide increased opportunities for state-of-the-art engineering courses for our engineering staff through paid university courses during the workday.

Sales training (example from cell A3)

The standard of marketing "value added": Within the next two months, all sales staff—account executives and support staff—will attend a workshop cosponsored by Engineering and Sales & Marketing to learn about features and benefits of our new products being introduced this spring.

The standard of solving customers' problems: As part of the orientation training for new salespersons, we will run a three-month mentoring program in techniques of problem solving, pairing up the new hire with an experienced account executive.

Systems training (example from cell A4)

The standard of networked offices: We will provide all office staff with eight hours of training on the new networked workstations.

The standard of standardizing hardware: The training organization will work with all managers to plan for the retirement or trade-in of obsolescent machines and to establish schedules for training on newly acquired machines.

Management training (example from cell A5)

The standard of keeping benefits under control: We will step up our program of training supervisors and managers to manage benefits, bringing down the level of control. More informed, accurate, and careful monitoring of employees' true needs should help solve the problem of skyrocketing benefits costs.

The standard of improving interviewing techniques: All managers will receive a copy of the new training video on Successful Interviewing to be used on their own time during the next two weeks. At the end of this period, a training facilitator will meet one-on-one with each manager for an interviewing role play to validate learning.

Customer service training (example from cell B1)

The standard of doubling the amount of repeat business: All customer service representatives will take the new course, Cultivating Repeat Business. Bonuses will be withheld until course completion is validated by the training manager and supervision.

Production training (example from cell B2)

The standard of identifying errors and defects: This company will embark upon an across-the-board program of information, training, and results monitoring to enable all production workers to find errors and defects during production processes instead of at the end of processes. The training phase will take two months.

Sales training (example from cell B3)

The standard of sales cost containment: Within the next month, all sales managers, support staff, and account executives are expected to take the new half-day workshop on cost containment developed by Ace Consulting Associates.

Systems training (example from cell B4)

The standard of efficient and effective hot-line responses:

The training department has developed a one-day field trip to four nearby companies that successfully operate efficient and effective hot-line functions. All hot-line operatives are encouraged to schedule themselves in this field trip on one of the five days during March when it is offered.

Management training (example from cell B5)

The standard of reducing overtime and reliance on temporary help:

All supervisors will attend the corporate workshop on time management and delegation during October. This is a newly revised work-shop that specifically addresses the skills you'll need to reduce overtime and use of temporary help.

Customer service training (example from cell C1)

The standard of time management on service calls:

Trainees will learn to improve their "time to satisfaction" by at least 30 percent as a result of taking the new course on time management for service representatives.

Production training (example from cell C2)

The standard of reduced accident rate:

Every safety course will build into it over the next six months at least 10 techniques for avoiding accidents.

Sales training (example from cell C3)

The standard of dealing effectively with rejections:

As part of orientation training, all new salespersons are expected to check out and study the training videotape on how to deal with rejections in cold calling. The training department will provide individual follow-up at one month, three months, and six months.

Systems training (example from cell C4)

The standard of 100-percent reliability: Software engineers are expected to take the two-day course, Software Reliability, developed by our team of visiting professors before they attend IEEE's regional conference. This course will be paid for by the training department if the course is followed by participation in a workshop on reliability at the conference.

Management training (example from cell C5)

The standard of accuracy in business projections: The training department is sponsoring a one-day off-premises workshop on how to do accurate projections. Managers are encouraged to bring actual examples of their projection challenges and problems to the workshop. The focus of this workshop is application of foolproof formulas and methods to the real problems of this business.

2. Samples of Standards for Administration of Training

How you run the training operation matters. The biggest mistake you can make is to allow training to be a reactionary, unfocused, undisciplined series of events that simply happen in response to being asked. Setting standards for the administrative functions of training operations will help you keep on track with all the vital underpinnings of good training.

These are some of the administrative functions to consider:

- Facilities management
- Production (word processing, art, printing, binding, packaging)
- Scheduling
- Registration
- Promotion and information management
- Media support (audio, visual, electronic)
- Computer systems support

To begin your thinking about stating administrative standards, review corporate goals and mission statements, especially those that directly or indirectly refer to more effective management practices and to "systems" support. Your company might have goals such as reducing the effects of massive retirements through enhanced educational opportunities for remaining staff, or leveraging the already existing knowledge base resident in current employees, or saving expense by making better use of in-house facilities. You might find a general admonition for all operations to cut to a certain computer record-keeping system by a certain date or for internal promotion regarding the company's personal and career development opportunities for all employees to visibly increase by a certain date. The wise training manager will be alert to the challenge of making training operations a proactive part of such goals.

The following section suggests several standards for each of the typical administrative operations of training. Use these samples for inspiration to develop your own standards.

Training standard

Facilities Management: Increased Visibility.	We will increase training's visibility by increasing the use of our conference room and media library by 80 percent during the next six months.
Production: Less Waste.	We will decrease the paper waste during training manual production by half during the next fiscal quarter by increased management monitoring of the point of document entry.
Scheduling: Timely Posting.	We will guarantee the timely posting of the master schedule by realigning the job duties of our three administrative assistants to reflect the inclusion of the new duty of posting the schedule at 10 key places throughout the company and updating our Web site.
Registration: Improved Efficiency in Paperwork.	We will embark upon a registration feedback and confirmation program during the next six months aimed at achieving a 90-percent "show up" rate at scheduled courses.
Promotion and Information Management: Equal Opportunity.	We will vigorously follow up each piece of promotional material to targeted groups within the company to verify that the target population in fact received and understood the communication from us.
Media Support: Respect for Individual Employees.	One way in which we will implement the corporate standard of Respect for Individual Employees is by decreasing by half our group-based classes and by doubling our

	self-paced CBT courses and video training programs.
Computer Systems	The training department will provide two
Support: A Personal	job aids, one in word processing and one
Computer on Every Desk	in database creation, to each employee
by the Fourth of July.	during the week prior to the arrival of his or
	her PC.

3. Layout of a Standards Document for Development of a New Course

Whether you choose to create a new course yourself or to hire someone to create one for you, you'll want to outline a development plan that is based on standards governing the *processes* of development as well as the *products* of development. Training managers often forget to establish process standards in their natural tendency to focus on the tangible results of development.

The layout shown in Figure 4-2 suggests the elements of process and product standards that can guide you and your staff during development of a new course. Use this layout so you don't overlook important elements of development—and important opportunities to state standards for this essential training department function. Standards can be created for each item in the list.

Figure 4-2. Layout of a standards document showing process and product standards.

Standards for Development of a New Course

Processes

- Time expenditure
- Verification of the need for the course
- Job and task analysis
- Writing
- Review (peer, management, customer)
- Run-through pilot testing
- Evaluation
- Feedback
- Revisions
- Printing and producing the course

Products

- Timetable for development
- Needs assessment document
- Learner objectives
- Learner evaluation exercises or tests
- Lesson plans and lessons
- Instructor manual
- Trainee manuals
- Graphics aids
- Handouts
- Media
- Review checklists
- Dry run or pilot test evaluation form
- Course evaluation form

Typical Application of Training Standards

The following case study shows how a large department store used the development of standards to move its force of retail clerks from a disconnected, lonely, unfocused, and independently operating collection of individuals to a focused, motivated, and cooperating team of employees. This case illustrates the vital role that training standards can play in a store's success.

Training Standards Foster Employee Empowerment

CONSUMER CAROUSEL is a family-owned department store that prospered for several generations in a small southern city. In recent years, the central city has declined in attractiveness and the store has moved from downtown to a suburban mall where it became the main "drawing card" for mall shoppers. The store expanded its lines of merchandise, added several departments, and hired about 30 percent more retail clerks and first-line managers.

At this time of growth, it became obvious that the personnel policies of the past that had served an older, more experienced, and more collegial downtown staff had to be revised—in a rather short time—to accommodate a need for the younger, inexperienced staff to present a unified front to the customer. Because the store retained most of its downtown work force, the challenge of integrating them into the new direction was also part of the task.

Continued on page 60

Continued from page 59

The new corporate standard was "to foster team spirit among all employees." The training organization immediately saw an opportunity to do some standard setting of its own to move the company rapidly toward its goals. Training standards looked like this:

- Involve all employees in setting a vision statement for their department, within the corporate standard of fostering team spirit among all employees and according to the five corporate business objectives for the next 18 months.
- Provide training in group goal setting, team building, giving and receiving feedback, and peer review processes.
- Work with various employee committees: Customer Satisfaction Committee, Employee Empowerment Committee, Sunshine Committee, and the Employee Recognition Committee. Include the goals and results of committee activities in the store's overall empowerment training by giving validity and visibility to the existing committee structure.
- Listen to others: Foster and facilitate an empowered working environment. Provide training as appropriate.
- Conduct bimonthly departmental "town meetings" that include back-office staff, managers, assistant managers, and retail clerks to identify problems and specify options for solving them.

Focus on the Issues

If you look closely at the standards, you'll find that something about each one can be "counted"—measured, ticked off on a frequency chart, tabulated, and reported as some approximation toward a specific goal. Measurement is the secret to standards that serve you.

In addition, this case addresses the specific—and classic—issues of the individual versus the team; the old employees versus the new ones. Standards can serve you well in these two classic struggles!

1. *Moving employees beyond demonstration of individual skills to performance as a team.* To tie in training standards with the corporate standard of fostering team spirit among all employees

means that training will have to be designed and presented in a facilitative and collaborative fashion. Training standards that reflect methods of achieving teamwork can help all employees to see the vision of change and to focus their behaviors on the challenging work of making the change happen. The training itself has to be a model for cooperation and mutual support.

2. *Using training standards as a vehicle for the new employees to embrace the old employees.* The standards that address giving and receiving feedback, group goal setting, working with existing employee committees, and listening to others provide authority for trainers and for employees—old and new— to keep working at all the basic human relations tasks that are so difficult to accomplish. Focusing on these kinds of standards can carry many a trainer through some rough times of being pressured to deal with results and bottom lines instead of human relations processes. The wise training manager will quickly get this kind of standard set down in writing so that this "soft" side of training is clearly tied to the corporate standard.

Setting the Measurement Mind-Set in Motion

Training standards, then, set you on a course of accountability. They give you guidelines for behavior and point toward the specific measures you'll need to use to evaluate your progress. They lay down the rules that will get you through frustrating and confusing times, and they will help lead you back on track when the pressures of immediacy try to overtake you. They function as your *Ten Commandments* and your *Bill of Rights!*

Chapter 5

Costs and Accountability

Being accountable for what you spend and why you spend it simply makes good sense. This is especially true in the growing business. When times are good, training is an important contributor to employee well-being and to profit. When times are not so good, training should be an important contributor to making them better. This can only happen, however, if the training manager has in place the accountability structure (realistic budgeting, accrual accounting, necessary and sufficient record keeping, program monitoring, and project management) that typically serves business well in the good times.

The Importance of Spare and Savvy Approaches

The biggest problem the training manager in a growing company faces is that often he or she is a one- or two-person management operation, and, although "the spirit is willing, the flesh is weak" when it comes to attending to the details of paperwork or data entry that accountability demands.

Even in large companies of 1,000 or more employees, training operations are often headed by a very small staff who must function as coordinators and instructors in addition to being managers. In such organizations, those in charge of training generally have a bent toward the "doing" parts of the job—the visible, human relations, customer contact, vendor management aspects of running training. Their sense of training management takes its shape from what they perceive as the special characteristics of the training or instructional function and their own frequent experience as instructors. Management in small training departments seems to gravitate toward gaining visibility for instruction, not for record keeping. Accountability seems like back-office number crunching, time-consuming drudgery that can wait until things slow down.

The reality of business growth these days is that it probably will not support expansion of training management positions within existing departments and those training managers in place will be expected to continue doing whatever it is that they now do. They will also be expected to behave like "mainstream" operational managers when it comes to planning, budgeting, auditing, and generally justifying their existence. People who manage training have to be especially careful not to commit organizational suicide by concentrating too inwardly on the nuts and bolts of training to the exclusion of the accountability exercises that keep other departments alive.

The corporate trainer at PHCS in suburban Boston is a case in point. She is essentially a one-woman show. Highly competent, politically astute, and very flexible, she maintains high visibility among her manager peers by being "totally available" to them and by being "very credible" in terms of quality and timeliness of training products and services. She says when she's ready, she'd like to hire a top-notch instructional designer and instructor combination—basically a clone of herself—so that she can "beef up" the behind-the-scenes strategic activities that she knows are essential to training's longevity and viability. In this rapid growth business where it's a heady experience to focus on the visible parts of training, this training manager understands the need to be efficient and savvy in accountability functions.

Growth these days is often seen as deepening relationships with existing customers and as pursuing greater quality in current products—that is, doing better and more with what you have. Tighter money, the aging of the employee base, and fiercer competition from home and abroad are realities that tend to focus the direction of growth away from the hotshot, get-rich-quick entrepreneurial spirit. Today's growing business demands training managers, who, like other managers, can boil things down to the essence and not necessarily depend on expansion and quantity to shape training practice.

Whether your company is riding the crest of a hiring wave or new market, or it is growing in service or quality by applying the principles of "small is beautiful," your management of the training function requires that you choose carefully the ways in which you justify your existence. In either case, you simply won't have the time to do all the accounting and record keeping that you know how to do. The following sections give you some specific help in choosing the cost and accountability structures that might make sense for your situation.

Figuring Out Whether to Make or Buy Training

One of the most important financial decisions you'll be faced with is the "make versus buy" decision. Factors in the decision include whether you can afford to pay benefits for additional regular staff, whether you'll have enough work to keep regular staff busy over the long haul, whether deep-down inside you trust outsiders, and, of course, whether you have good talent available to you either for hire as staff or as consultants.

The following suggestions can help you with the financial considerations in the decision to make or buy training:

1. Consider that designing and producing a course from scratch takes time. One month of design and development time is required for one day of classroom training; at least one day of instructor preparation time is needed for each day of training.

2. Don't ever try to write your own course unless you have an experienced instructional designer working with you. Technical writers, software documentation specialists, engineers, and R&D types generally do not automatically make good course designers although they are bright and logical. Consider hiring an instructional design consultant for a short time if you can't afford a full-time instructional designer.

3. Consider buying generic training, especially for management training. It is generally not worth the effort to design and develop courses on, for example: how to delegate, good communication, effective presentations, interviewing techniques, managing performance, time management, back safety, and English as a second language. Shop around and preview several packages to be sure the information is relevant, current, and adheres to your company's standards regarding racial and sexual bias. Be sure that the "organizational culture" of the manuals and/or audiovisuals matches your own organizational culture.

4. If you don't have any instructors on staff, buy courses and the instructors to go along with them. Chances are that a vendor will provide you with a more experienced instructor than one you might be able to quickly run through your own train-the-trainer program.

5. Create your own course if your company's business is highly competitive or highly proprietary in nature. For example, if you have unique systems, high-tech products, new services, or new R&D technologies, don't risk trade secrets leaking through tem-

porary employees or consultant course designers. Make your
own courses by using your own loyal employees, not outsiders.

6. Whenever you hire an outsider to create training for you, be
sure to establish and stick to a monitoring and formative evaluation plan of design reviews and product inspections as the
work progresses. Be sure that you get error-free work. It's far
less costly to catch problems early during development than to
find you have a finished course full of problems that is scheduled to be given to paying customers tomorrow.

Creating Alliances

"Leveraging" is a word that has become one of the hottest new
elements of business vocabulary these days, especially as it refers
to both saving money and increasing opportunity for growth. We
hear of leveraging knowledge of employees throughout companies,
leveraging customer intelligence, leveraging diversity and cultural
differences around the world, and leveraging community facilities
and resources. The idea of making resources at hand work so that
everyone wins—that is, of creating alliances and partnerships for
mutual benefit—is an idea whose time has come.

Perhaps the most obvious example of partnering in training is
seen in the numerous arrangements across the country between
businesses and community colleges. A long and important article
by David Stamps in *Training* magazine, December 1995, entitled
"Community Colleges Go Corporate," details the activities of many
community colleges throughout the United States. (Find David
Stamps at Lakewood Publications in Minneapolis at 612.333.0471.)
Stamps reports case after case of alliances that have worked for big
companies—like between Motorola and Maricopa Community College in Phoenix, Arizona, or between Sony and Symantec and Lane
Community College in Eugene, Oregon—as well as for small companies with community-based missions that happen to fit nicely
with the community-based mission of their neighborhood community college. Leveraging the education function of the community
college and its community development charter can be an ideal
solution to a local business's need for a particular kind of training.

There are cautions, however, and any training manager needs to
be alert to some of the pitfalls. Pricing varies. One community college charged $100 per class hour—inexpensive by any standards—
enabling a company to run a 15-hour training program for $1,500.

Another community college charged $250,000 for a contract to do pre-employment training for 200 prospective employees. The estimate for 1995 was that the top 50 community college "contract-training" programs across the country averaged about $1 million in annual fees. Quality varies too. Stamps cautions corporate trainers to be wary of a college professor/classroom mentality and of community colleges that insist on classes being held at the college location. Community colleges that come to your business site are much more cost-effective for you, and have a much greater chance of delivering the "need to know" kinds of learning services that transfer to the job more quickly. Stamps cautions against faculty who have never been out of the classroom, and argues for more flexible staffing arrangements whereby external/contract training consultants, for example, partner first with the community college and then are placed on business assignments. Leveraging the availability of business-based independent consultants and the flexibility of community college administration can be a winning proposition to local businesses. As in all kinds of training, however, be clear about your objectives for the learner and buy carefully.

The American Association of Community Colleges, Washington, D.C., estimates that at least 90 percent of the 1,200 community colleges in the United States offer some kind of contract training to local businesses. Trainers who want to get involved with their community college should look first to see if there is a contract-training division that can be responsive to your specific need. You need to be wary of those schools that simply have a continuing education division that offers "nice to know" courses on their campuses. Look for staff persons who will come to you and listen to what your practical needs are and who talk the language of "just enough and just-in-time"; stay away from professors who grudgingly agree to make space in their classrooms for some of your employees. Realize that there are few standards or consistent models for delivering partnership or alliance-type training services, and that there are probably as many programs out there as there are community colleges and businesses. If you're looking for long-term relationships and alliances, start early to establish instructor competency standards, spell out equal access issues and guidelines, and be sure that both college and company accounting practices are followed. Community college programs are funded by a variety of state, federal, and local sources, some with programming constraints. Most funding sources are very egalitarian and broadly constituted to serve the community served by the community college. The administrative, programming, and pricing flexibility are all benefits of leveraging the availability of the community college; they can also present a few hurdles, so be advised before you seek a training partnership.

The community college near my home is NORTHWESTERN CONNECTICUT COMMUNITY-TECHNICAL COLLEGE (NCCC). In a visit to the college during the preparation of this book, I picked up some college documents—brochures and catalogs—describing NCCC's various programs. What I found there is illustrative of the great flexibility, community-building mission, and variety of learning experiences that are possible through the community college. What's important to the training manager trying to get some good training going is that chances are there's someone at the local community college who can help, and there's some kind of program structure, funding source, or already developed program that might work just fine for you.

Northwestern Connecticut Community-Technical College's comprehensive catalog spells out its educational philosophy, and includes these words: "the meaningful connection between classroom and the rest of the world"; "the College expects each student to receive the education essential for him or her to make an effective contribution in his or her major field of interest." Its institutional objectives include: transfer to four-year colleges and universities, preparation for employment, general education, community education (cultural, social, recreational), special services specifically "designed for and offered to area businesses and industries," and student support services. Clearly, this is education with the adult student's interest and need at its center; like company training, the educational philosophy is a real-world approach. The community college and local business make an ideal partnership. Check the library of your own community college for its catalog and program brochures.

Specifically, some of the kinds of things NCCC offers that could readily be adapted for use by a local business are: certificate programs in purchasing management, Web design, supervisory skills, software applications, and graphic arts. NCCC's specialized Continuing Education catalog suggests that these certificate programs might be just the right approach for the adult student who is "entering the world of work and needs to minimize the time that is spent in the classroom." Many courses already developed by the college are offered for CEU credit, often an incentive that can be offered by an employer to a company trainee. NCCC runs a heavily used Academic Skills Center where students can drop in or schedule one-to-one tutoring in basic math and communication skills, as well as in academic subjects like chemistry, biology, psychology, or art. The college's Center for Student Development offers "career planning, job placement, counseling for deaf and disabled students, services for Veterans affairs," and other counseling and referral services. A busy English as a Second Language program and a GED/high school equivalency program are also ongoing standard fare, and, in fact, the college is currently collaborating with a local training manager to provide ESL instruction to company employees. A Tech-Prep program aimed at skill-building for high school students focuses on a broad liaison between those likely to be entry-level workers and the range of learning opportunities available through the college's programs. Any of these kinds of programs and services could be replicated or adapted for success in a business setting. With careful investigation and planning, the business/community college partnership can be a great cost-saving, an effective service, and a successful learning opportunity.

Other Ways to Save Costs Through Collaboration

Other kinds of collaborations, not necessarily under the administration of a community college, are also possible as a way to minimize costs in a newly developing training operation. Pay particular attention to government programs through the U.S. Department of Labor, to state-developed programs using federal funding flowing from work force legislation frequently run through state departments of education or of labor, and to programs offered by the Small Business Administration, the U.S. and local Chambers of Commerce, and through local community or regional organizations unique to your particular area.

A case in point is the Workforce Investment Act of 1998, Public Law 105-220, which reforms current federal programs for job training, adult education and literacy, and vocational rehabilitation. It consolidates more than 70 federal job training programs and provides states with the responsibility and flexibility to create work force development programs in partnership with local (municipal) governments. The law calls for the establishment of "Work Force Investment Boards" made up of local business leaders. At the center of the legislation are one-stop service centers to provide job seekers with career counseling, skill assessments, training, job search assistance, and program referrals. "Individual Training Account" vouchers are available for qualified individuals to purchase training services. Local as well as state efforts will be evaluated against standards for success in job placement, retention of individuals in jobs, earning gains for individuals receiving jobs, and skill attainment of individuals who have received training. All states must implement PL 105-220 by July 1, 2000. New training managers are well advised to check out this source of various training-related, community-based services, and to keep watch for other kinds of federal jobs–related legislation. Volunteering to be a member of such a board can also be a useful kind of partnering. Program materials alone that emanate from this kind of massive legislation can be enormously helpful as guidelines for initiating your own monitoring and measurement activities.

Another federal source of business training is the Corporation for Business, Work, and Learning of the U.S. Department of Labor. A program near my home called Berkshire Enterprises, using $220,000 in grant money, has trained more than 800 individuals in how to develop a successful small business and provided assistance to more than 400 small businesses. Among the skills that program participants learn are: how to develop a business plan; how to do market research, promotion, marketing, and sales; and how to find financing and manage money. The Small Business Administration, addressing a similar need, has recently opened six Women's Business Centers across the country to provide services, referrals, and, most of all, funding sources to help women small business owners to succeed. (Check this out online at www.sbaonline.sba.gov.)

An obvious source of inexpensive collaborative help is the local library. Don't forget the power of books! Libraries can often be persuaded to order copies of books that are particularly useful for what your company needs to know; libraries can also often be persuaded to offer quick courses on using the Internet, and to organize book-based study groups of various kinds. Libraries may also be persuaded to develop a business video collection that could be used by your business as well as other businesses in the region. Along the same lines, it may be possible to create your own in-house learning resource center housing books, videotapes, audio tapes, and various company-standard software programs for trainees to check out and use for self-study at their own pace. This can be done with minimal clerical staffing and minimal expense, at the same time it creates a training presence in the company. Along with self-study comes the informal one-to-one kind of information and resource sharing that colleagues do naturally at work. Capitalize on this human tendency and give it some structure such as a "Bag More Than a Lunch" weekly noontime sharing session where folks come intentionally to pick each other's brains about work issues and problems as they eat their lunches.

And of course, don't overlook membership and involvement in a local professional association such as ASTD for monthly stimulation and sharing of ideas and resources. Talk with your peers in other companies; share ideas, resources, and even facilities. (For the location of a local chapter of ASTD near you, phone the international office at 703.683.8164.)

Also, get wise to the typical management fear that training will take up too much time and take employees away from the real business of the company. Use computers to distribute information to the desktop and the workstation; save training time by using online technology and databases. Take information dissemination out of the training function and save hours and even days of "training" time. Much of classroom training time is taken up by passing information around; move this function to the desktop where it is immediately usable, and keep training time and the necessary interactivity of person-to-person learning for its true instructional purposes. Look for alternatives to classrooms full of trainees: collaborate with line managers and frontline service employees to do the training at the employee's workstation. Get the manager's help in designing and delivering the training. Make training look like working.

Untangling Costs and Benefits

Trainers like to believe that the appropriate measure of training success is the dollar value of improved performance minus the cost of training. The only problem in most companies is that nobody has the time to keep records about the dollar value of improved performance.

For example, we know in a general sense that lower turnover in a retail sales force gives us a better shot at higher performance, based on less money and resources invested in new hires, and it generally also costs us less in terms of the training dollar spent. Shop floor supervisors can tell us that a particular production problem is costing us plenty of money in rejected items, low morale, and absenteeism, and that several kinds of training might be indicated. However, those same

---

supervisors can seldom take the time to document the variables that go into "costing out" increments of improved performance, and the prescribed training never even has a chance of being able to prove its worth in hard, cold cash. Account representatives who are responsible for initial training of customers on a newly delivered device can digest the folder full of customer feedback forms and know that the customers were generally unhappy with the "turnkey training" they received and lacked the confidence to proceed into full application of the new product. But "frown tests"—or "smiles tests"—don't assign dollar amounts to the lack of performance by the account representatives, so there's no way of figuring out how training those sales folks to be better customer trainers might contribute significantly to the company's ability to keep its customers and promote its products. In most companies, the costs and benefits of training are difficult to nail down.

What this suggests is the importance of cooperation between training managers and other managers in establishing the right financial measures so that everybody counts the same things in the same ways. Bosses and program auditors are often happy to point out that training costs a lot of money—in consultant and vendor contracts, media costs, travel and living expenses for seminars, and the lost opportunity costs of spending time in class instead of on the job—but they are hard pressed to quantify the cost of the unattained benefit. Training is frequently outmaneuvered into a defenseless position regarding cost and benefit analysis simply because nobody has paid any attention to consensus on evaluation methods. Without agreement on the measure and methods of cost-benefit analysis regarding productivity and training, training managers will never be able to claim their legitimate successes and promote their direct contributions to the company's financial health. Training always loses when the only numbers you can produce are the person-hours of classes taken or average head cost per trainee per vendor-delivered course. These training numbers mean virtually nothing in terms of performance benefits to the company as a whole.

Figure 5-1 shows a simplified cost-benefit analysis. It assigns a dollar value to the problem, to the solution, and to the result. It is an example of a cost-benefit analysis that results in a dollar figure for training. Critics can argue that such an analysis merely presents the reader with cost utility data, not program effectiveness information. They'll tell you that qualitative measures are good enough when it comes to measuring training. On the other hand, supporters of cost-benefit analysis will tell you that the "rosy glow effect" is an insufficient conclusion about training and productivity and what training really needs is discipline and a hard focus on measured impact. Training managers in the growing business will have to decide whether it's worth their time and energy to professionalize the management of training by systematically using the same financial management tools as other managers use.

Several resources are available: *Workforce* magazine has an online service called "Valuing Training" in its Trends and Resources section. Find current information on return-on-investment (ROI) of training programs here: http://www.workforceonline.com/trends/previous. ASTD's Information Center staff is particularly helpful and can fax information to you within a few hours. Phone them at 703.683.8184. Also, check ASTD's Web site, http://www.astd.org.

Figure 5-1. A simplified cost-benefit analysis.

Assigning a Dollar Value to the Problem

• 500 rejected devices at our manufacturing cost of $40 each	$ 20,000
• Foreman's extra hours in troubleshooting time 30 hours @ $30	900
	$ 20,900

Assigning a Dollar Value to the Solution

• Vendor course Building Quality In for three principal lineworkers @ $200	$ 600
• Salaries of trainees "lost" during training ($400 x 3)	1,200
• Consultant plan for follow-up monitoring	500
	$ 2,300

Assigning a Dollar Value to the Result

• Within two weeks of the end of the course, 80-percent decrease in rejected devices	$ 16,000

Cost-Benefit Analysis Calculation

• From the point of problem definition, a cost of		$ 20,900
Value of the benefit	$ 16,000	
Less cost of the solution to the specific problem	$ 2,300	
• Net benefit		$ 13,700

Another way to think about cost-benefit analysis is to take the long-term view of the benefits accrued from seminars attended, college courses reimbursed, and technical skills developed in formal training programs. At some point, your educated and skilled employee base will pay off for you in terms of better and more lucrative contracts, ability to create new products and new markets, individual increases in productivity, and more effective and efficient management. At some point there will be a "crossover" point at which the investment costs in training will level off and the benefits will take over. IBM, for example, calls itself a "learning company" and invests heavily in training. Management believes that "in the long run, success will accrue to the quickest, smartest and toughest-minded" (*IBM 1990 Annual Report*).

A simplified version of this thinking is to assign a cost figure to a learning curve of, say, 50 percent of first year salary. If training costs for that employee that first year can reduce the learning curve, training can save both a percentage of lost salary and recruitment costs because employees can become more productive earlier in the year.

Dr. C. W. Hoover Jr., Professor of Engineering at BROOKLYN POLYTECHNIC UNIVERSITY in New York, told me that

> return on investment in the continuing education of engineers is very high for most firms even if it produces only a small increment in productivity (measured by additional engineering effort available). The analysis can be done using the firm's own income statement and shows that a firm can pay an increment for education that is a large fraction of the engineering budget and still break even, even if the education produces only a small increment in productivity. All of the assumptions are conservative. If this is the case, it is likely that the payoff will be greater than break-even for reasonable investments.

The trick in this long-range cost-benefit analysis is to identify exactly what you will count—time intervals, dollars, sales, percentages, frequencies, net income, gross income, margin—and how you will go about counting. A graphic representation is shown in Figure 5-2.[1]

[1.] A more complete version including the analysis is published in the proceedings of the IEEE Careers Conference as *Return on Investment in Engineering Education,* Sixth IEEE-USA Careers Conference.

Figure 5-2. Long-range cost-benefit analysis.

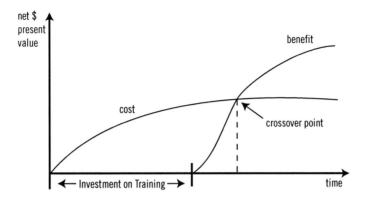

Source: C.W. Hoover Jr., National Academy of Engineering, *Focus on the Future, A National Action Plan for Career-Long Education for Engineers.* Washington, DC, 1988.

Another approach to establishing benefit or value is to think of average performance as the top midpoint of the bell curve and each deviation from average as one standard deviation. By equating average performance to, say, a dollar figure representative of salary, one can then assign a dollar figure to a standard deviation and calculate the cost of less than average performance or the value of more than average performance. Statistically speaking, about 70 percent of all scores fall within one standard deviation of the average (mean).

Obviously, the tough part is assigning a number to the effect of training, so that it can be used as a multiplier for the value assigned to the standard deviation. This is possible, of course, with prior discussion and agreement among management staff regarding the definitions of these variables. Any equation, naturally, has to include the number of trainees, the cost per person for training, and a payoff interval of weeks or months.

Why the Smiles Test Isn't Good Enough

The "smiles test" is the affectionate name given to the usually simple, one- or two-page feedback form that trainees fill out at the end of a course.

The problem with the smiles test is that it focuses too narrowly on only instructional delivery and excludes the rest of the training function. The worth of training should not hinge on whether or not the trainees liked a course. Smiles-test feedback forms can often be no more than a popularity contest for instructors or a particular training room, or a course's personality profile. More often than not, the standard feedback form tells the person in charge of training very little about cost-effective changes that could be made in the course. It gives you very little meaningful information to translate into dollars and cents and communicate to other managers, controllers, and bosses.

Most enlightened training managers have been able to move training beyond buying an off-the-shelf course and presenting it to a group of trainees. Training departments, even small ones, generally try to incorporate the functions of analysis, design, development and production of materials, delivery of instruction, and evaluation. Training managers think in terms of costs for each of these major functions of training, and not just in terms of purchased courses and instructors' salaries.

A more meaningful evaluation of training should include a variety of measurements, checklists, feedback forms, monitoring checkpoints, and tallies that address each of the functions of training: analysis, design, development and production of materials, delivery of instruction, and evaluation. If training managers find themselves in the position of having to trim the operation to save costs, they should look for savings in each of these functional areas. It's always possible to find less expensive analysis methods, tighten the design process, tweak development person hours, effect savings in production materials and processes, find cheaper classrooms or alternative delivery methods, and make the results of evaluation activities more immediately useful. When smiles-test feedback forms are the only "hard data" available and the focus of evaluation narrowly remains on the delivery of the course, the training manager is hard pressed to zero in on what can be changed throughout the operation to make training both better and more cost-effective.

Audit and Program Evaluation

When *Forbes* staff reporter Peter Fuhrman wrote in the April 1, 1991, edition of the magazine that Operation Desert Storm rendered the Soviet Union's $30 billion investment in arms used by Iraq "fit only for scrap" and its warfare training theory and methods obsolete, he was doing a gross audit and program evaluation. His article goes on to describe why its training and technology failed, and concludes by pointing out that the Soviet Union's 20-percent defense budget (compared with 6 percent in the United States) is "a terrible drain on the economy."

Observers—auditors, accountants, controllers, vice presidents—to the training operation in a growing business very often go through the same kind of thought process as the *Forbes* writer did. This is cost-benefit analysis thinking, or accountability thinking, and it's based on defining the costs in real dollars.

Training managers who begin their overall program assessments through this kind of accountability thinking can often claim a large expenditure figure. For example, at the spring 1990 field trip of ASTD's Connecticut Chapter to IBM's Management Development Center, the host training manager reported that "last year IBM spent $1 billion for education," not including travel, living expenses, and salary of trainees ($2 billion if these costs were included). Each day at IBM, there are about 20,000 people in company-sponsored education and training classes or programs. IBM believes that it's worth it.

IBM believes in education and training, runs the operation as a cost center, and allocates costs back to operational units as a percentage of each unit's head count. This is a growing company that has set up its accountability structures and measures according to its philosophy of doing business. IBM and other growing companies in which training operates as a cost center often engage in self-study or audit exercises during which the training manager determines costs of major parts of the training operation.

Most companies that run classroom training as the primary instructional delivery mechanism find that delivery—including instructors' salaries, materials used by instructors and trainees, the use of classrooms, and instructional support staff salaries—costs about 30 percent of the program budget. Development costs often average out at about 10 percent to 20 percent of the budget—even in organizations where it takes 40 or 50 days of development time to produce one day of classroom instruction. ASTD's Benchmarking Forum companies in 1997, the last year of data collected, showed an increase in the amount of money spent on outside services including design, development, and delivery of training. According to ASTD's 1999 State of the Industry Report (Summary), 76 percent of companies used outside providers. A whopping 50 percent to 60 percent of the total cost is often made up of trainee salaries and travel and living expenses. Most training managers are always on the lookout to find ways of reducing that 50 to 60 percent drain on the effectiveness side of the equation, including using outside services in creative ways to minimize high expenses traditionally associated with classroom training.

Persons in charge of training simply have to know where to go within their organizations to produce dollars and cents numbers that can tell mainstream business observers—bosses, controllers, other managers, customers, stockholders—how the program is contributing to the company as a whole. To do this, obviously, you have to know what parts comprise your program, what these parts cost, and what you're contributing to productivity, quality, profit, or any other overall business goal.

Good Advice from an Internal Consultant

Hans Brouwer is head of Management and Organization Development at a 15,000-employee public transportation bus company, VSN-1 PERSONENVERVOER, in The Netherlands. He is one of a growing number of international associates of ASTD, and was generous in talking with me about how he faced and solved some management challenges in his business. His comments are good advice for those in charge of getting a training operation started in a mid-size business with a multilevel hierarchical management structure.

Hans Brouwer functions as an internal consultant to management on the broad subject of organization development, including training. His is a somewhat wider perspective—one that reflects America's and his company's interest in "performance" and not just training. He is concerned with innovation in a typically non-innovative kind of business, with continuous learning, and with alignment of training with corporate operations. These are his comments to help you facilitate successful training department beginnings in your company:

1. Pay attention to top management's planning and control cycles, and be sure that you get your training plans and resource needs into those cycles. Guard against operating on your own timetable; first do your homework about how top management budgets, plans, and makes decisions.

2. If your company is a "bottom-up" company, allow plenty of time for frontline trainers and developers to have adequate input of ideas before your department plans and budget make their way upward to top management; realize that innovative programs take more time to shape in a bottom-up company.

3. Avoid training jargon when you talk with ordinary people who just might be in powerful decision-making positions in your company; use favored, commonly understood words like "performance" and "learning."

4. Use outside organizations like colleges to train and recruit new trainers; for example, Brouwer teaches a train-the-trainer course at a local university in hopes of creating a well-positioned training worker pool for his and other companies.

Advantages of Managing Through Accountability Structures

It should be obvious to you that well-managed training means that you run training with the same business know-how as you would run any other major function of business. The foundation of managing well is accountability in dollars and cents terms—accountability that is tied to the highest-level business goals of your company. These are the advantages of being accountable as you develop your training program:

- Your budget process parallels that of the company as a whole.
- You become proactive and assertive as a business operation, not always on the receiving and responding end.
- Any other manager, and your boss, can understand your accounting. You value what they value in dollars and cents.
- Your reasons for requesting resource help seem logical and reasonable when they're backed up with no-nonsense records.
- Standard management tools, principles, and ways of operating clarify the benefits of what others often consider a "warm fuzzy" operation.
- When you're due for a salary increase, the reasons for it will be obvious.

Tools for Managing the Costs of Training

The seven tools in this chapter show you how to do the cost accounting, budgeting, and financial management of training. Box 5-1 contains a brief summary of the seven tools discussed in depth in this section. Five budgeting tools, an audit preparation tool, and a project management tool are presented in easy-to-use fashion meant to clarify what can be a confusing job fraught with many not-so-clear options. Particularly in budgeting, there are many options for record keeping and reporting; these tools give you the framework for making good decisions about how you deal with your fiscal responsibilities as the person in charge of training.

Box 5-1. Tools for managing training costs.

1. *Proposed Budget Summary Form*—Like the executive summary of a business plan, the budget summary is the document that top management reads from top to bottom

2. *Detailed Budget-Building Worksheet*—A sample backup information sheet to show you how to develop and document each budget item as you build your total budget

3. *Alternative Functional Budgeting for New Training Departments*—An alternative budget form reflecting a process of accounting by the five major functions of instructional system design (ISD)—analysis, design, development and production, instruction, and evaluation

4. *Budget-Building Guidelines*—Guidelines for companies of 100, 500, and 1,000 employees as you build fiscally responsible training

5. *Accrual Accounting Forms for Tracking Your Budget*—Two forms that keep track of what you're spending and what you have left in each of your accounts— record keeping that makes next year's budget preparation much easier

6. *Audit Record-Keeping Checklist*—An invaluable checklist for the inevitable day when someone "up there" (the controller, the CEO, or your boss) says it's time to take a look at the total training program, helping you get it all together quickly

7. *Project Management Guidelines*—A simple explanation of what training project management is all about

---

1. Proposed Budget Summary Form

The form shown in Figure 5-3 is created as a summary document for the detailed budget worksheets that follow. This Proposed Budget Summary would probably be the top page of your various budget preparation worksheets. It is the form that will be placed next to other managers' forms on the boss's conference table when he or she sits down to allocate resources throughout the company. The right column, Approved Budget, is where your boss will write in what your budget will be. (The worst thing that you can do is to simply apply a multiplier across the board from this year's current budget to the proposed budget.) Check your current tax guide and with your company accountant for the correct account titles.

Figure 5-3. Sample proposed budget summary form.

Proposed Budget Summary

Effective date of proposed budget _____

Name of department _____

Manager's name _____

Code	Account Title	Current Budget	Proposed Budget	Approved Budget
1000	Salaries			
2000	Benefits			
3000	Purchased Services			
4000	Supplies			
5000	Capital Outlay			
6000	Other			
	Total			

Example

Two categories, Salaries and Purchased Services, are illustrated below. Be sure to develop, with input from your company controller, a list of all items in each major code category.

1000	**Salaries**
1111	Professional full-time
1112	Professional part-time
1113	Secretary
1114	Training specialist, assistants

2. Detailed Budget-Building Worksheet

All good summaries are backed up with detail sheets. The sample worksheet in Figure 5-4 shows you how you might arrive at a dollar figure for audiovisual equipment. As you see, all the essential decision factors are included on the detailed budget-building worksheet. Use this type of detailed backup sheet before you transfer the "total" to the proposed budget summary form.

Figure 5-4. Example of a detailed worksheet to be used in arriving at a total for the proposed budget summary form.

Detailed Budget-Building Worksheet

Code and Account Title   <u>5120, Audiovisual equipment for trainee use</u>

Priority key

1 = essential   A = addition

2 = highly desirable   R = replacement

3 = desirable

Priority	A/R	Description	Unit Cost	Quantity	Cost Total
1	A	Overhead projector	$2,500	1	$2,500
1	A	VCR/TV 13"	600	4	2,400
2	R	Canon copier (upgrade)	3,000	1	3,000
				TOTAL	<u>$7,900</u>

Code	Account Title	Current Budget	Proposed Budget	Approved Budget
5120	AV equipment	$6,500	$7,900	

3000	**Purchased Services**	3117	Telephone
3111	Instructor services (vendor-delivered courses)	3118	Power
		3119	Water
3112	Instructional design services	3120	Cleaning services
3113	Evaluation services	3121	Equipment maintenance
3114	Graphics and artwork	3122	Advertising
3115	Printing and binding	3123	Staff travel
3116	Copy services		

3. Alternative Functional Budgeting for New Training Departments

Another way to build a training department budget is to organize your operation into "program" or "function" categories. Examples of functional areas or programs of the training operation are:

A.   Analysis

B.   Design

C.   Development and Production

D.   Instruction

E.   Evaluation

This could be a useful way to approach budgeting, especially if you are just beginning to build a training department—either because you're new as a training manager or because your company is growing. Each functional area contains the standard account code items such as salary, benefits, purchased services, supplies, etc. Budget forms are similar to those previously illustrated, with the addition of the function identifier.

The disadvantages of using this approach are that you get into assigning percentages of time (reflected in salary and benefits accounts, for example) and fractions of usage (reflected in capital outlay and supplies, for example). When your fledgling department is made up of you and your secretary, it's hard to decide if you are 0.25 of your salaries in design and 0.75 in instruction, or some other somewhat arbitrary breakdown. Your budget preparation worksheets can get rather full of decimals and "full-time equivalents."

On the other hand, the advantages are that you can set your operational goals for each functional area, allocate budget for each one, and then track your expenditures on a periodic basis through program or functional accounting. This kind of budgeting and accounting can help you see where your total program strengths and weaknesses are and ultimately decide when and in which functional areas to expand or cut back. The functional alternative version of the proposed budget summary might look like the one shown in Figure 5-5.

Figure 5-5. Proposed budget summary form (functional alternative).

Proposed Budget Summary

Effective date of proposed budget _____

Name of department _____

Manager's name _____

Functional/Program Area: B		Design		
Code	Account Title	Current Budget	Proposed Budget	Approved Budget
1000	Salaries			
2000	Benefits			
3000	Purchased services			

4. Budget-Building Guidelines for Companies with 100 to 1,000 Employees

There is no magic formula or standardized dollar figure to apply to a training department's budget. Corporate giants like Xerox, AT&T, or Ford Motor Company have annual training budgets in the millions of dollars, and often are so decentralized that they don't even know what they spend on training. On the other hand, a company of 50 or 100 employees often "does" training with virtually no budget.

As in other management functions, how you deal with training management depends on your philosophy of the role of management. Most managers believe that their role is that of planner and establisher of control; they believe that management is not a haphazard, reactionary, "sniff the wind" kind of endeavor. This book suggests that you are better off subscribing to the planning and control school of thought in training management and provides you with tools to shape your operation with these roles in mind. The trick in planning and control is to be reasonable, not to go overboard with plans, analyses, and reports, and to recognize and manipulate the variables in the total training operation so that efficiency, effectiveness, and quality come through in your people, your products, and your services.

Although there are unknowns regarding optimal budget figures—because everybody's objectives are different—we do know for sure that skilled employees who understand their jobs and their companies contribute more and faster to making their companies grow. Whether you are a big or a small company, growing slowly or more rapidly, there are some general budget-building guidelines you can adapt to your own situation. These will be followed by suggestions for companies of various sizes: up to 100 employees, up to 500 employees, and up to 1,000 employees.

General budget guidelines for all training managers

The following guidelines will help you plan and control your budget.

1. Estimate the total number of employees who will take a certain course over a two-year period. Figuring the costs and benefits on as long a time base as possible, up to two years, is a generally workable guideline. Continue to do an annual budget, but allocate half of your figured cost to one year and the other half to the second year. Costs will be less if you can anticipate and plan for reruns over a two-year period. You'll save on analysis, design and review time, course materials, and instructor prepa-

ration time by looking at a two-year baseline. This approach is especially relevant to CBT and interactive videodisc (IVD) courses that tend to be expensive per trainee.

2. Don't skimp on instructional design and development time and salary if you choose to create your own course from scratch. Consider doing this yourself if you have sensitive information, intellectual property, proprietary software, or highly competitive products. In this sort of company, big or small, it will pay you in the long run to hire a high-level instructional designer to work with your technical professionals or product managers to create, field test, and evaluate courses just for your company. Allow a course developer or instructional designer at least one month to create one day of classroom training—that is, a three-day course could take three months to get off the drawing board if only one person is assigned the task of development. Person-days is the metric.

3. During design of a new course, insist on design reviews at frequent periodic intervals to catch errors before they get built into the course. Involve representatives of all significant audiences for the course in the design reviews—probable trainees, probable instructors, managers who might eventually pay to have their people take the course, suppliers, customers, etc.

4. If you have inherited a group of courses from a previous training manager, take a good, hard look at each one to see if they can be shortened. Pay attention to course evaluation forms from trainees, and be sure to ask all previous instructors of the course if they think the course could be shortened. Most courses contain extraneous information and can be tightened. Reread the objectives of the various lessons; you'll generally be able to see the parts that aren't quite on target or perhaps even out-of-date. Hours trimmed mean trainees spend less time away from their jobs, and you'll be able to do more with the budget.

5. Allow some time for analysis, but be sensitive to what you call this analysis period in your budget. Most other managers will be eager to accuse you of "analysis paralysis," so be careful—a little goes a long way when attaching dollars to it.

6. Put some teeth into your evaluation or don't bother. If you expect to learn anything from evaluation, consider doing a variety of evaluation activities—for example, questionnaires, structured interviews, reviews of course objectives and content before you begin writing the complete course, focus groups

---

with other managers to review your program as a whole. Also consider budgeting a small sum for a third-party evaluator—another manager from within the company, a local college professor, or an independent evaluation consultant—who can give you some assistance in designing evaluation objectives and instruments and help you interpret the data you collect. Paying attention to evaluation is an especially good idea if you've been given the green light to start a new training operation or if you are involved in a major change, such as a merger of several human resource functions or taking over after a retirement.

7. Figure out what business you're in as a company and as a training operation and develop a training budget that reflects that business. Trim out any training that doesn't focus on the heart of your business. Forget the management training in this year's budget if your management force has stayed the same as last year and has already taken all the management courses you have to offer. Don't get caught in doing the "nice to knows"—"need to know" is what it's all about. Remember President Jimmy Carter and Zero-Based Budgeting? It's a very good idea when it comes to developing the annual training budget.

Dealing with budgeting as an ongoing activity of good management

No matter what size your company is, no-hassle budgeting flows from the following steps:

1. Find out what line managers really need, talk with them about what you can do for them and together with them for the company, and get their support for your approach before you go about the specific task of budgeting.
2. Set objectives for the training operation as a whole.
3. Develop a plan to achieve each objective. Plan specifically.
4. Forecast costs and expenditures necessary to carry out your plan in its specified time allotment.
5. Present the formal budget document and get it approved.
6. Keep current records regarding encumbrances and balances; administer the budget on a continual basis.
7. Evaluate the budget regularly (for example, monthly) in relationship to your training operation objectives.
8. Communicate your progress and problems to those who can be helpful to you. Be realistic, open, and corrective as the year progresses. Don't wait until the end of the year to rejoice or to panic.

Getting the big picture through training benchmarking

ASTD's Vice President for Research, Laurie J. Bassi, heads up a division with staff and associates who provide numerous member services in the form of studies and reports. One such service, personalized training benchmarking, provides anyone who chooses to participate with comparative data on ratios such as training expenditures per employee, training as a percent of payroll, percentage of employees receiving training, employees per full time equivalent trainer, amount spent per employee on trainers' wages, and training payments to outside companies as a percentage of total. These key ratios reflect the important cost and budgeting issues as we approach the millennium: effects of downsizing on staffing, training as a strategic player in corporate growth, training as investment, and trends toward outsourcing. More than 800 organizations have participated in this study, with more added all the time. (Find information about the benchmarking service through ASTD's Web site, www.astd.org; share information with the benchmarking service through e-mail at benchservice@astd.org.)

Related to this is ASTD's Benchmarking Forum, a consortium of organizations that engage in benchmarking of training, learning, and performance improvement. From time to time, reports from this forum are shared with membership at large. Both of these efforts are a part of ASTD's current, scientifically sound, ongoing research program to support leadership in the field of training and performance.

The January 1999 issue of *Training & Development* magazine contains "The 1999 ASTD State of the Industry Report," authored by Bassi and Mark E. Van Buren, and its summary, "Sharpening the Leading Edge." The focus here is on leadership—what leading-edge training operations do, as well as what the rest of trainers do. Like no other survey, the ASTD survey tells the reader what needs to be done to be part of the significant leading edge.

Budget realities in companies of varying sizes: 100, 500, and 1,000 employees

Training magazine also publishes annual surveys of trainers' salaries and many other reports on training expenditures and budgets in October and November of each year. Data below come from the "1998 Industry Report" in the October 1998 *Training* magazine, the "17th Annual Salary Survey" in the November 1998 *Training* magazine, and from ASTD. (Go online to check out current salary information at www.trainingsupersite.com/salary/.)

- Training staff salaries make up nearly three-quarters of the total training operational budgets.
- Working in a big company ($500 million in annual sales) will get you the most salary. Training managers with five or more full-time trainers reporting to them earn the most pay.
- Women training professionals in 1990 made an average salary of $39,000; men made an average salary of $53,000. In 1998, women training executives averaged $75,000; men averaged $88,000.
- A master's degree or Ph.D. will get you up to $10,000 more in salary per year.

Overall training budgets increased 3.6 percent over the last year.

- Leading-edge companies outspent other companies in training by 2 to 1: $300 versus $150 per employee.
- Companies with fewer than 500 employees represent about 80 percent of the universe of training operations.
- Companies with fewer than 500 employees spend nearly as much on outside services, seminars, and products as do companies with 10,000 or more employees.
- Generally speaking, as a human resources professional you're better off financially in training than you are in personnel, especially if you're in management training or technical training. Trainers' salaries are up 20 percent since 1993, but lag behind other managers.
- Payments to outside training providers increased 20 percent between 1996 and 1997; if you are an outside provider, that is certainly good news.

In terms of general budget practices, ASTD estimates that U.S. companies invest only 1.8 percent of payroll in training—far less than Japanese or European companies—and that this training reaches only about 10 percent of the U.S. work force. ASTD currently recommends that 3 percent of payroll be allocated for training (ASTD "Benchmarking Service Report 1997," and ASTD "1999 State of the Industry Report" in *Training & Development*, January 1999). ASTD's benchmarking studies contrast these averages with the current practices of companies that are making conscious efforts to improve. Some typical budget realities are presented in Figure 5-6.

Figure 5-6. General budget practices for training expenditure.

Overall Budget	Staffing	Outside Services and Products	Facilities and Equipment
100 Employees or Fewer			
• Your major budget items are a percentage of your salary and your secretary's salary and benefits. • You have funds to send about 10 employees to seminars or conferences. • You buy a few books and several training videos.	• You probably spend only half your time on training; your title reflects this. • You probably also share a secretary or assistant.	• You probably hire outside consultants and vendors and spend most of your nonsalary budget on purchased training videos and one- or two-day seminars. • Technical workers get training; managers probably don't.	• You have a small office and no training room. • You run classroom training in a borrowed conference room or maybe the cafeteria. • You rely a lot on on-the-job training. • You probably have an overhead projector, a VCR, a TV, and a copy machine.
Up to 500 Employees			
• Your major work is coordination work, although you do some design and development work. • Your budget includes materials production and equipment maintenance. • You have a small training library of magazines, books, and reports. • You belong to ASTD or some other national training organization.	• Your title probably reflects that 100 percent of your time is spent on training, but quite possibly you are not a full manager. • You probably share a secretary, unless you do customer training or regulated safety training, and then you probably have your own secretary or training assistant. • You run train-the-trainer programs to help line managers and technical professionals do one-on-one training.	• If you are a professional services company or an R&D operation, you probably are working on creating one or two courses in-house from scratch, and it's probably you who are doing the writing. • Your outside budget probably includes money to send people to seminars on quality methods, and perhaps on management topics.	• You have a small office and workroom. • You have a training room for classroom training that's generally well equipped and dedicated only to training. • You probably have a personal computer and some graphics software for producing your own training presentations. • You have a training library, probably on a shelf in your office or workroom.

Continued on page 90

Continued from page 89

Overall Budget	Staffing	Outside Services and Products	Facilities and Equipment
Up to 1,000 Employees			
• You have to figure on charge-back accounting two ways—what other departments owe you when you train their employees and what you owe them when you use a "lateraled" employee as an instructor. • You run a train-the-trainer program. • You have a library and conference budget.	• You are a training manager or director with your own secretary. • You might have one instructional designer or combination instructor-instructional designer reporting to you. • You have technical experts reporting to you occasionally when they have to become instructors. • You have one or two training specialists who look after AV materials, registration, and promotional services.	• You send people to conferences and seminars, and you buy vendor and consultant services. • You design and produce about half of your own courses. • You buy ready-made courses off the shelf and modify them.	• You have one or two training class-rooms. • You buy videos. • You buy several VCRs and TVs. • You have at least one cubicle with a VCR-TV for independent study. • You have a PC with graphics and desktop publishing capability for doing your own AV materials, manuals, catalogs, newsletters, and promotional materials.

Another way to look at budgeting

Within the article by Nancy Kuhn, "Training from Scratch," in *Training & Development,* October 1998, is a sidebar by Ryann Ellis, ASTD's interactive communications coordinator in the Information Services operation. Among other things in her sidebar entitled "The Nuts and Bolts," Ellis suggests a simple formula for determining the internal cost of training: **People x Hours x Salary.** She also provides some current guidelines regarding percentages of resources:

item of budget	percentage of resources applied
participant time	30 – 45 %
training staff	10 – 20 %
preparation time	2 – 10 %
external consultants	15 – 30 %

training space	5 – 15 %
visual aids	2 – 10 %
off-the-shelf materials	5 – 10 %
travel and accommodations	3 – 10 %
evaluation	2 – 10 %

This listing of items is based on a training operation that is largely focused on delivering training in classrooms, either on site or off site. Classroom delivery is still the overwhelming choice for delivery of training, as numerous national reports at the beginning of calendar year 1999 indicate. This "Nuts and Bolts" chart reflects that reality.

5. Accrual Accounting Forms for Tracking Your Budget

After your training budget has been approved and your fiscal accounting period begins (usually a year, but sometimes less in a new training operation), you'll need to carefully track the depletion of your funds. To do this, set up a file folder or computer file called *Budget Tracking.* Figure 5-7 shows a sample budget tracking form.

Figure 5-7. Budget tracking form (accrual system).

Budget Tracking Form				
Acount Number	Approved Budget	Encumberances	Payments	Unencumbered Balance

In accrual accounting, as soon as a purchase is made or purchase order signed, the obligation is charged to the "encumbrances" column of the tracking form. The same account number is used here as in your detailed budget preparation worksheet. When the bill is paid, you credit that account with the original encumbrance and charge the final payment to it. By doing the double entry, you'll always know how much is actually still left in your budget.

In addition to the file folder of budget tracking forms, it's also a good idea to prepare a periodic "budget performance report." A quarterly report is a good interval with which to start. An example of such a report is shown in Figure 5-8. In the first column of the report, you list the categories or account numbers. Expenditures for the current period and year-to-date are recorded in the next two columns. In the last two columns at the right, you report the over-budget (in parentheses) or under-budget status of each account for the current period and the year-to-date.

Figure 5-8. Example of a periodic reprint of expenditures in the training budget.

Training Budget Periodic Performance Report

Period   3 months: 1Q, 2Q, 3Q, 4Q   Year

Account	Actual		(Over) Budget	Under Budget
	Current This Period	Year-to-Date	Current This Period	Year-to-Date
1000	3150	5400	(80)	(250)
2000	1200	3000	100	150
3000	—	—	—	—
4000	—	—	—	—

6. Audit Record-Keeping Checklist

These are some of the records you'll probably need to produce during a training department audit:

Records Needed

☐ Annual proposed budget and approved budget
☐ Periodic budget performance report, for example, encumbrances, actuals, year-to-date figures
☐ Staffing chart, job descriptions, and staff credentials
☐ Department program objectives, e.g., financial objectives such as proposed margins
☐ Courses offered
☐ Class rosters, including department titles and the names of the managers who paid the training bills
☐ Catalogs, bulletins, and promotional material
☐ Plans, e.g., business plans, timelines, and expansion plans

- [ ] Training expenditures as a percentage of payroll
- [ ] Training cost centers, summarized, e.g., customer training, on-campus courses and programs, CBT and IVD training, independent study center
- [ ] Evaluation study results and description of methods
- [ ] Trainee feedback comments
- [ ] Instructor feedback comments
- [ ] Staff performance review documents
- [ ] Memoranda for record or your own self-evaluation documents
- [ ] Agreed-upon format for the audit report

7. Project Management Guidelines

Very often in training, you initiate a self-supporting or profit-making project in addition to your regularly budgeted items. "Things" happen during the course of doing business: you want to run a seminar to make use of a big name consultant who, you just found out, is going to be in your area for a national meeting; your favorite course manuals and books got moldy in storage over a particularly steamy summer and need to be replaced; you want to take advantage of a computer manufacturer's promotional deal but you'll have to plan for some in-house training, as well as the purchase of the hardware.

These guidelines are specifically directed to the training manager who wants to run a special project on top of the regular training budget:

- Define the project "deliverable" (product or end result)—for example, a new course, a conference, an orientation videotape, an environmental safety curriculum, a supplier certification training job aid, a computer simulation training course.
- Scope out the project, assigning persons and deadline dates to each task. Authorize one person to be the project manager, and set the project team members in motion.
- Estimate costs in person-days, supplies, overhead, and purchased services; project the profit you expect to realize.
- Lay out a monitoring plan with roles, responsibilities, and relationships spelled out; specify the format and time intervals for communication and documentation about the project. Have frequent project team meetings and encourage feedback and corrective actions as the project progresses.

Choosing Project Management for Accountability

The following case study outlines the development of a training project at a consumer products company with branch offices in several major cities across the United States. This project was above and beyond the existing train-the-trainer course, which had gotten "stale." The company's corporate training organization had remained stable for about a decade; therefore, the direction of growth in internal staff training—including train-the-trainer training—was to grow in depth.

The corporate training manager decided to treat the development of this new, advanced train-the-trainer course as a project, thereby subjecting the development process and the course itself to the accountability structures inherent in project management.

Development of Advanced Train-the-Trainer Course Using Project Management

This course was designed in advanced-level instructional modules that could be "mixed and matched" according to individual trainee needs over a period of five days plus two evenings. Daytime modules included objectives and instructional theory, instructional methods and classroom management techniques; there were also laboratory modules in skill practice, performance and competency demonstration, and evaluation. Evening modules focused on electronic delivery systems.

Development of this course required the following project accountability controls:

1. Project Deliverables
   - The project plan
   - Student guide
   - Instructor guide
   - Visuals and graphic aids
   - Case study examples
   - Demonstration guidelines and procedures
   - Models and solutions
   - Exercises and tests
2. Project Phases (including a person responsible for each phase)
   - Verification of needs
   - Instructional design
   - Development and production of materials
   - Field testing

3. Development Quality Assurance
   - Creation of development standards for each phase
   - Time schedule and cost estimate for each phase
   - Evaluation and feedback against standards, schedule, and cost for each phase
   - Estimation of lapsed time and total time requirements of both professional staff and support staff

Focus on the Issues

This case was chosen because it illustrates a situation that is very common in the growing business. This is the situation where something comes up that has to be financially accounted for outside of the regular budget. It has to be planned, managed, staffed, funded, and monitored above and beyond the carefully budgeted items and planned developmental activities.

When something comes up, for whatever reason, the accountability scheme known as project management can handle the extra burden on your human and fiscal resources. It is often the accounting structure of choice for a growing training operation in a growing business.

The other issue that this case addresses is the kind of growth that a stable or perhaps aging work force faces. This issue is illustrated here because companies of all sizes need to know how to guide and account for this kind of growth in the decade ahead.

These, then, are the two issues illustrated by this case:

1. *How to account for development above and beyond the norm.* The additional development effort above and beyond the existing course required tighter controls than the routinely scheduled development efforts of the corporate training department. Because an existing course was in place and had served the staff for many years, the development of a new course on the same subject was somewhat suspect to a number of old-time employees and other managers. Project management accountability structures provided tight controls for this development effort.

2. *How to account for growth in depth.* Growth in depth requires an accountability system that isolates and accounts for the unique features of development efforts and products that foster growth in depth. Project management's focus on deliverables, phases, and quality assurance provides this compatible system.

The Choice Is Yours

As you prepare to initiate and implement an accountability system for training, focus on the benefits that your training programs will provide for your company. Look to the end results of what you do; don't get caught with your head in the sand looking inward. Accept the challenge of making the training operation an active contributor to productivity and profit, and execute your leadership through training accountability systems that other business leaders can understand.

There's no single magic accountability formula or one right way to do it. The choice is yours to seek the advice of your company's accounting department, to keep good financial records (not just smile forms), and to communicate with other managers and company executives about the costs and benefits of training. How you do all these things will vary from situation to situation; that you must do these things is a constant of good business practice.

Chapter 6

The Business of Employee Development

The growing business takes on employees in order to stay in business. Although employment is an agreement among persons who trust each other and have each other's interests and mutual goals in mind, it is first and foremost a contract between parties who agree to support each other for work and for profit. Employee development should be seen as a business decision that will contribute to the company's mission, goals, and plans.

Those who will be working 10 years from now are probably all currently on the payroll. Our employee base is aging, there are fewer young workers available, and the number of new jobs is growing more slowly and more skewed than in past years. In addition, American employees are more diverse now than in the past and are continuing to become more diverse. They will require longer periods of time to become acculturated into mainstream patterns of performing work.

Research by many organizations confirms this. For example, the much publicized Hudson Institute reports, *Workforce 2020* (1997) and *Workforce 2000* (1987), researched by ASTD's Laurie Bassi, Scott Cheney, Anthony Carnevale, and associates throughout the 1990s, and numerous other labor and employment studies elaborate on the aspects of workplace demographics and their effects on the human resource base of American business. Quite simply, these demographics demand that companies invest time, energy, and training resources in developing their current employees because these are the ones who'll be dealing with the challenges of change at the millennium. Human resources development can no longer expend most of its budget in recruiting and hiring. The real human resources challenge for growing companies as the turn of the century approaches is to provide the existing employee pool with extensive knowledge, skills, and value systems through training.

Human Capital as the Competitive Edge

Strategic economic thinkers tend to view the employee base in American businesses as human capital, capable of actually figuring into the nation's productivity formulas and results, as well as centrally affecting national profit and loss calculations. Training for our human capital development falls into two essential categories: (1) the specific training that an individual company pays for and provides to its employees who use it for this company only and (2) the general training that is paid for by an individual company, but which is ultimately useful to many companies. In practice, according to human capital theory, what happens is that companies generally pay higher wages following training in order to minimize their risk of turnover and keep tighter control over their own investments in the human capital, which they deem important for their own growth.

Productivity is often seen as the ratio of output over input, where input includes all the expended resources (training included) that are required to enable an employee to perform well. The treatment of human capital in terms of numbers and ratios like this makes it a factor in investment strategy in many companies. Obviously, training must be designed and delivered well so that the input denominator of the fraction contributes to a higher productivity result. At the management level, employees' jobs must be designed better, so that the fit of worker to job is tighter. At the public schooling level, more communication between school teachers and business leaders has to occur, curriculums need to be changed so that children and teenagers come to school prepared to think, to solve problems, and to work together for common goals. In short, the invested inputs to the productivity formula (productivity = output ÷ input) at all levels of employment readiness must be made less costly in terms of potential training required.

Relating the high-level theory to the practical realities of employee development in a growing business is not as hard as it might seem. The NOACK ORGAN COMPANY, a small, growing, internationally active, high-quality, very specialized craft shop, actively searches for employees who have succeeded in work demanding similar thinking skills and similar motor coordination skills that organ building requires. Noack, the master organ builder, essentially cashes in on what academics call general training investment—that broad-based training provided by other companies and educational institutions to people who eventually became Noack employees—training that he did not have to invest in. On the other hand, Noack invests in on-the-job training by allowing his employees to make mistakes. In his kind of business, problem solving and learning from mistakes in a collegial environment with common and clear goals pays off. That kind of specific training, although not training in the traditional sense, provides his business with the opportunity for lower input training costs and consequently higher productivity. His human capital base becomes his competitive edge.

A Dun & Bradstreet study of small businesses (*The Challenges of Managing a Small Business,* 1989) looks at the Noack approach as a motivation issue (p. 19). In this study, several business owners discussed the importance of encouraging and guiding employees in key management activities that help to build and retain a competent staff. Allowing good people to make mistakes, according to one owner, and turning those mistakes into a "positive" helps people settle into the work of the company and to believe in themselves. Employees need experiences at work that make them feel they "belong," give them feedback that they are valued, and enable them to contribute to the common good.

The ultimate increase in productivity depends in a very real sense on the accumulated ways in which business owners and managers of work invest in their human resources. Dun & Bradstreet estimates that more than 90 percent of American businesses employ 50 or fewer employees. ASTD found in its 1999 benchmarking study that most companies train about 74 percent of their employees. Studies formerly cited by ASTD indicate that employees who receive formal training on the job earn at least 9.5 percent more and as much as 25 percent more than those who have not had training. These statistics surely indicate that human capital development can be a powerful strategic competitive tool and that a lot of work needs to be done. Boosting a company's dollar commitment to training seems to make sound long-term economic sense—for corporate growth and profit, the economic improvement of American society, and the individual employee's well-being.

The recent good news for employees in America's 6 million-plus organizations with 500 or fewer employees on the payroll is that they typically receive as much training as employees in companies with more than 500 employees (Cohen, *Training & Development,* April 1998, pp. 27-30). The bad news is that only about half of employees at the low-wage/low-education level in all types of companies received training, raising questions about employee development as equal opportunity and about training as a vehicle for supporting economic growth (ASTD "1999 State of the Industry Report," *Training & Development,* January 1999).

Policy Options Behind Employee Development Issues

There is a real concern among U.S. policymakers that our work force is fast becoming low-skilled and low-paid. Reports from many sources throughout the decade estimate that at least 20 percent of American young adults aged 21 to 25 read at only an eighth grade level; in the early 1990s, many companies of all sizes came to grips with workers' inability to read and write and offered basic literacy courses. In the late 1990s, states began the push to certify more literate public school teachers. The 1998 "mid-term" elections countrywide focused on education.

In an effort to stem the costs of training, many managers "dumb down" the work—reduce jobs to their simplest tasks. The unsettling result of these trends and the profile of the work force is that American skills will not be able to support a globally competitive set of industries or an improved standard of living. Congress through its Office of Technology Assessment (OTA) has been justly concerned. It would indeed be a national disaster for the costs of training to drive a further widening of the gap between the skilled and the nonskilled, the rich nations and the poor nations, the haves and the have-nots. Congress's 1998 debate on the H-B1 work visa extension for highly skilled foreign workers reflects the concerns that developed earlier in the decade.

In the early 1990s, OTA identified 16 policy options at the federal level to address training issues (*Worker Training,* 1990, pp. 42 ff.). These options are listed under four major issues:

1. Reducing barriers to firm-based training
2. Retraining individual workers for career advancement
3. Linking training and technology assistance
4. Improving the quality and effectiveness of training

Among the most widely discussed options is that of a national training levy—a mandated percentage of each employer's payroll to be committed to training its own employees or to be paid into a national or state training fund. ASTD's benchmarking study in 1998 estimated that U.S. businesses spend only an average of 1.8 percent of payroll on training. ASTD recommends, at minimum, that we increase this to an annual commitment of 3 percent of payroll, with a goal of 4 percent of payroll. Australia, for example, in July 1990 instituted a 1 percent of payroll national training levy, known as the Training Guarantee Scheme, and increased it to 1.5 percent in July 1992.

The chart shown in Figure 6-1 lists OTA's 16 options for the U.S. government's involvement in training.

Figure 6-1. Summary guide to federal policy issues and options regarding commitment to training.

Issue Area A—Reducing Barriers to Firm-Based Training

1. Help firms set up training consortia.
2. Expand technical assistance to trade association, others.
3. Consider limited tax credit for private-sector training.
4. Phase in payroll-based "national training levy."

Issue Area B—Retraining Individual Workers for Career Advancement

1. Expand apprenticeship concepts.
2. Adequately fund federal support for vocational programs.
3. Fund workplace basic skills program.
4. Provide favorable tax treatment for continuing education.
5. Evaluate ways to help finance workers' continuing education.

Issue Area C—Linking Training and Technology Assistance

1. Coordinate technology and training assistance.
2. Help states expand industrial services, combined with training.
3. Support creation of an employer institute for work-based learning.

Issue Area D—Improving Quality and Effectiveness of Training

1. Encourage adoption of best practice approaches and technologies.
2. Fund the federal training technology transfer program.
3. Fund more civilian-sector learning research/technologies.
4. Improve the information base on work-based training.

Source: U.S. Congress, Office of Technology Assessment, *Worker Training: Competing in the New International Economy, OTA-ITE-457.* Washington, DC: U.S. Government Printing Office, September 1990, p. 43.

Leadership for Employee Development

Obviously, it takes time for federal initiatives and overarching goals to turn into practice. The immediate work of using training as a strategic and personal employee development tool falls on the shoulders of the person in charge of training.

Development is different from supervision; development goals should be differentiated from salary increases. Employee development requires training managers (and supervisors) who:

- Shape visions and inspire employees to achieve
- Represent and interpret the company culture and work environment to individual employees
- Intervene directly in employees' performance improvement both for short-term and long-term growth

Leadership in training requires, above all, the ability to *connect* employees. It requires a lateral focus in addition to a top-down focus; it requires broad networking on behalf of employees in addition to narrowly analyzing an individual's performance profile. Training leadership for employee development requires creating and presenting many opportunities as well as zeroing in on and facilitating what an employee's personal strength is. The secret to effectiveness in employee development efforts is to combine your skills in personnel administration, supervision, and training technology in some mix that encourages, empowers, and instructs.

Building Teams

These days, training operations are also responsible for facilitating the building of teams. Teams of all sorts—permanent, non-permanent, flexible, highly structured, cross-functional, self-determining, ad hoc, competitive, non-competitive, and all sorts of variations on any of these arrangements—are filling our workplaces. American business for nearly all of its existence as a force in our kind of economy has been organized to reward "the lone ranger"; our hero has generally been the "Marlboro man"–type of rugged individual with steely eyes set on the mountaintop in the distance. Until recently, we have valued independent achievement over group or team achievement—a nation of independent strivers seeking individual success. In the 1990s, particularly, this ideal changed to a focus on the work of teams and their success. Interdependence and not independence permeates business language.

It is useful for trainers to think of a team as a collection of individuals with individual learning needs first, then as a group entity with group needs for learning, all wrapped up in one package. We have included three tools in Box 6-2 (presented later in this chapter) specifically to help you orient your thinking toward teams, team learning, and team performance. The following section on behavior engineering also can help you see the value of interconnectedness and interdependence in facilitating high performance in an organization. Employee development means more than working with an individual's gaps in knowledge, skills, or attitudes.

The Concept of Engineering Human Performance

Tom Gilbert and his followers believe that worker performance can be codified and "engineered" so that improved performance occurs as a predictable result of interventions. Gilbert is sometimes called the father of performance technology, and his book, *Human Competence: Engineering Worthy Performance* (McGraw-Hill, 1978), has become a standard reference on the subject. Gilbert's Behavior Engineering Model is a three by two matrix that classifies six major factors in both the work environment and an individual that can be addressed in a scientific way in order to improve performance. Gilbert's model (see Figure 6-2) suggests that the manager can focus on any of these cells in the matrix in an attempt to develop—and not just remunerate—employees.

Figure 6-2. Gilbert's behavior engineering model.

Behavior Engineering Model

	Information	Instrumentation	Motivation
The Business Environment	1. Data	2. Tools and materials	3. Incentives
The Individual	4. Acquired knowledge and skills	5. Innate capacity	6. Needs and desires

Source: Adapted from T. Gilbert, *Human Competence: Engineering Worthy Performance* (New York: McGraw-Hill, 1978), p. 88; and the International Society for Performance Improvement (ISPI), (Washington, DC: 1996). Reprinted with permission of ISPI. See complete original model in Chapter 10, Figure 10-1.

Gilbert's point, and the emphasis of performance technology, is that there are elements other than the employee's motivation and ability that come into play in that person's demonstration of effective work behavior. A human resources professional who is concerned with employee development must analyze all the factors that affect behavior—those in the organization or business environment as well as those of a more personal and individual nature. Often small investments of money, time, or other supports in any one of the six factors can provide the leverage that results in improved actions.

Training itself is generally reserved for the fourth factor in the matrix, that is, when a gap is discovered in an individual's knowledge or skill about the job. The wise training manager will try to separate out the training solutions from the other possible solutions to inadequate performance. If you can do this, you'll be on the right track to *develop* your employees—using training, of course, but also using other human resources interventions targeted at other performance deficiencies. Knowing when to use training and when not to use training is probably the most important piece of intelligence you can have as a training manager in a growing organization.

Advantages of Using an Employee Development Approach

Throughout the United States, companies are rediscovering the enormous potential in individual employees. They're investing more in the most desirable workers, and are laying off the ones who are not needed any more. Leaner work forces are being expected to produce higher-quality goods and services. Training plays a pivotal role in serving individual workers, and an employee development (rather than a "document the mistakes") approach is the approach of choice for this smaller and more challenged work force. The following list contains some of the major advantages of adopting an employee development approach at your company.

- Planned sequential learning can occur.
- Objectives for individuals can be set that separate training for knowledge, training for skills, and training in values and attitudes—objectives for each person are differently defined.
- Individual competency, performance, and career growth can be addressed in an organized way.
- Employee development can be monitored and measured using criterion-referenced measures, maximizing individual growth.

- Employee development can minimize the risk of turnover, cut down recruiting costs, and enable employees to be happier at work doing a job for you.
- Employee development focuses management efforts on investment in human capital—in the end, a business's unique and most valuable asset.

Tools for Developing Employees

Eight tools in this chapter have been chosen for their usefulness in helping you focus on the developmental needs of individual employees. The tools are summarized in Box 6-1. The detailed discussion, charts, checklists, and forms that follow will make it easier for you to meet your employee development needs through training. The clue here is to work through line managers or supervisors who know their employees best.

Box 6-1. Tools for employee development.

1. *Knowledge, Skills, and Values Chart*—A simple chart suggesting a gradation of learning tasks in the three major categories of education that helps you separate an employee's training needs

2. *Know-Yourself Checklists: Employee's Career Path Analysis*—A useful tool for an employee to use alone, prior to meeting with you

3. *Employee's Career Path Profile*—An employee job satisfaction scale with biographical information that can figure into training plans to be completed by the employee

4. *Supervisor's Career Path Assessment*—A form to be completed by an employee's supervisor, specifically tied to skills required to do the job and the employee's status relative to the skills; specified training needs for this employee during the next 24 months

5. *Employee Skills Evaluation*—A job-monitoring form for developmental use by a supervisor ranking skills according to importance to the job and the employee's performance

6. *Employee Development Plan*—The individualized training program for an individual employee

7. *Leadership Checklist for Employee Development*—A guidance tool for you and your company's supervisors

8. *Employability Checklist*—15 ways to learn on the job from work itself to keep yourself employable

---

1. Knowledge, Skills, and Values

Most jobs contain task requirements of varying difficulty. Most jobs also contain a combination of requirements in the areas of knowledge, psychomotor or neuromotor skills, and attitudes and values. Obviously, people are integrated entities, and their knowledge, skills, and values cannot be neatly separated—for example, without adequate knowledge, higher-level skills cannot be demonstrated. However, it is useful in training to think of an employee's development requirements in terms of these classifications because each of these categories of on-the-job behaviors can be taught and evaluated differently. In fact, over the last several decades, educational psychology research has concluded that excellence in one of these domains doesn't necessarily mean excellence in the others—for example, smart (knowledgeable) people don't necessarily have a superb set of values. When you are trying to develop employees, it is helpful to think about the requirements of that employee's job so that you can pinpoint that person's specific areas of strengths and weaknesses. Employees can and should be developed differently for the various requirements within their jobs.

The following chart will help you distinguish among the three basic categories of behavior in order to begin to design a development program for each employee. Several examples of lower-level and higher-level behaviors are given to jog your thinking. The examples are based on the classic works of Benjamin Bloom, Elisabeth Simpson, David Krathwohl, and Bertram Masia. (See the Bibliography at the end of the book.)

Behavior Categories

	Lower Level	Higher Level
Knowledge	Identify	Translate
	Label	Rephrase
	Define	Interpret
	Recall	Evaluate
	List	Plan
Skills (motor)	Touch	Connect
	Place	Build
	Wait	Modify
	Smell	Straighten
	Sit	Reconstruct

Values	Attend	Prefer
	Receive	Conceptualize
	Respond	Characterize
	Accept	Value
	Choose	Commit

2. Know-Yourself Checklist: Employee's Career Path Analysis

The form shown in Figure 6-3 can be useful as a self-assessment tool for your employees to use prior to any career development discussions with you. Employee development, of course, is a two-way deal. Be sure that you give your people an opportunity to hold up their end of the bargain. Their own self-analysis will be helpful to you as you zero in on the requirements of the job and then create a development program based on any discrepancies between their own assessments and yours.

Figure 6-3. Employee career path self-assessment tool.

Know-Yourself Checklist: Career Path Analysis

To the employee: Prior to career path or job advancement discussions with your supervisor, review this checklist by yourself. Use the Comments column to record any ideas that can jog your memory or help you focus your thoughts. Take this checklist with you to use during discussion with your supervisor, and leave it for your supervisor to forward to the training manager. Knowing yourself and being able to articulate this knowledge to others are often the keys to successful career planning and advancement.

This information will be shared with the training manager in order to maximize opportunities for your growth and to improve the work of this company.

Self-Assessment Questions	Comments
1. What results do I want?	
2. How much recognition do I need?	
3. How much energy do I have?	
4. What factors release my energy?	
5. How does the working environment affect me?	
6. Do I work best alone or in a group?	
7. How do I respond to criticism?	
8. What do I do to turn others off?	
9. Am I a good listener?	

Continued on page 108

Continued from page 107

10. Do I work slowly or quickly?	
11. Do I like to learn?	
12. What is my best learning style?	
13. What do I value on the job?	
14. Can I give and receive feedback?	
15. Do I like to compete?	
16. Why should the company value me?	
17. What are my personal goals?	
18. Do I prefer to lead or be led?	
19. What are my weaknesses?	
20. What are my strengths?	

Source: C. Nilson, *Training Program Workbook & Kit* (Paramus, NJ: Prentice Hall, 1989). Reprinted by permission of the publisher, Prentice Hall, Direct A Division of ARCO.

3. Employee's Career Path Profile

The career path profile shown in Figure 6-4 is another tool for the individual employee to use when engaging in self-analysis regarding his or her own career path. Often, it helps employees who are seeking advancement or greater job satisfaction to be confronted—in written form, in black and white—with the factors that contribute to promotion and job satisfaction. Any development program must consider the factors in individual job satisfaction, because, of course, they vary from one individual to another.

Figure 6-4. Employee career path self-analysis profile.

Employee Career Path Profile

To the employee: This Career Path Profile will be used to help you progress beyond your current level of productivity through training opportunities during the next 24 months. Please complete the profile and return it to your supervisor by _____, 19 _____.
Within two weeks, your supervisor will review your responses and meet with you to discuss the completed Career Path Profile.

Biographical Information

Name	Date

Job title	Social Security number

Highest degree or diploma

Number of years in current job   Number of years in this company

---

Desired job within 24 months

Job Satisfaction Information

Place an X on the rating scale after each item indicating your satisfaction with that item.

	Dissatisfied	Mildly Dissatisfied	Neutral	Mildly Satisfied	Satisfied
1. Pay					
2. Benefits					
3. Bonuses and awards					
4. Promotion policies and practices					
5. Job description					
6. Working conditions					
7. Relationship with peers					
8. Support from supervisor					
9. Computer and systems support					
10. Clerical and staff support					
11. Career guidance					
12. Professional growth opportunities					
13. Training opportunities					
14. Recognition					

Source: C. Nilson, *Training Program Workbook & Kit* (Paramus, NJ: Prentice Hall, 1989). Reprinted by permission of the publisher, Prentice Hall Direct A Division of ARCO.

4. Supervisor's Career Path Assessment

The form shown in Figure 6-5 is a tool to be used after the employee has completed his or her own self-assessment regarding career path and job satisfaction. This assessment is tied to the skills required to do the job and indicates the employee's status relative to these skills. The assessment by the supervisor zeroes in on skill needs and proposed training to meet those needs. It also focuses on the job that the employee desires two years in the future. This document provides the outline of an individual development plan based on training.

Figure 6-5. Career path assessment tool to be completed by the employee's supervisor.

Supervisor's Career Path Assessment

To the supervisor: Please complete this Career Path Assessment indicating your assessment of this employee's skill levels and training needs for the next 24 months. These data will be used to improve training and enhance productivity. This assessment is intended to be used after discussion with the employee regarding the Employee Career Path Profile. Please forward to the training manager by _____, 19____.

Employee's name	Date

Supervisor's name

Employee's current job title/classification

Employee's desired job within 24 months

Employee's relevant prior training or testing

List of Required Entry-Level Skills for Desired Job	Employee's Skill Status		Training Suggested During Next 24 Months
	Yes	No	

Source: C. Nilson, *Training Program Workbook & Kit* (Paramus, NJ: Prentice Hall, 1989). Reprinted by permission of the publisher, Prentice Hall Direct A Division of ARCO.

5. Employee Skills Evaluation

The evaluation form shown in Figure 6-6 is another tool for the supervisor's use. It is specifically intended to help an employee perform well in his or her current job. Special features of this form are (1) a list of skills required for this job, (2) a rank ordering of each skill in importance to the job, (3) a rating of the employee's current performance on each skill, and (4) brief notes made by the manager to support the current performance rating of each skill.

This employee skills evaluation is not meant to be a replacement for the annual performance review. This tool is intended to be a helpful development tool, not a "file" document supporting or denying promotion or salary increase.

This skills evaluation is especially useful as a retraining development tool. It can help the supervisor and training manager who are faced with the need to meet the challenge of changing times with a static employee pool. When doing the list of skills required for the job, be sure to think in terms of the knowledge, skills (motor), and values categories. Employee development is enhanced when both the employee and supervisor are clear about the true nature of the job requirements. After this kind of an evaluation, many employees and their supervisors realize very quickly where the problems are and can readily see a clear path of development to address the identified skills gaps.

Figure 6-6. Skills assessment tool to be used by the employee's supervisor.

Employee Skills Evaluation

Employee's name _____ Job title _____

Supervisor's name _____ Date _____

Skills Required for This Job	Importance in Rank Order (1 = least to 4 = most)				Performance Rating (1 = low to 4 = high)				Observation Notes
	1	2	3	4	1	2	3	4	

6. Employee Development Plan

Use of the development form shown in Figure 6-7 follows completion of the Employee Skills Evaluation Form (Figure 6-6). This form also focuses on current skill performance. This form is the development plan for an individual employee. Of course, it is backed up with details of the action items and their costs in dollars and time: for example, in-house courses, outside seminars, field trips, videos, books and periodicals, on-the-job training, mentoring opportunities, college or adult school programs, and professional association memberships.

This plan begins with transposing from the previous form any skill in which the employee requires development—a skill that is weak or perhaps one that is strong and can be enhanced by very high-level training. The plan includes the specific program or action that addresses the skill development need, a probable time in which that program will be accomplished, the person responsible or a contact person associated with that particular program, and a notation of when that program was actually completed. This development plan should be created by the employee and supervisor with guidance from the training manager.

Figure 6-7. Employee development plan with a specific program of action.

Employee Development Plan

Employee's name			Job title	

Supervisor's name			Date	

Skill	Program	Time	Contact	Completion

7. Leadership Checklist for Employee Development

Finally—or perhaps initially—the supervisor or training manager needs to focus on his or her own leadership behaviors when it comes to employee development. The following checklist is an effective guidance tool for you and your company's supervisors.

Leadership Checklist for Employee Development

Shape visions and inspire employees to achieve by these actions:

☐ Facilitate employees' abilities to feel and act like leaders.
☐ Recognize employees for their contributions.
☐ Tell everybody what your goals and strategies are.
☐ Get the right people on your side early.
☐ Don't be a wimp: stand up for what you believe in.
☐ Create plans that can be adjusted; know your options within your strategic focus. Be flexible in implementation, but firm in values and goals.

Represent and interpret the company culture and work environment to individual employees.

☐ Generate enthusiasm for your employees' work and its contribution to the company's mission.
☐ Build upon your upper management network and your understanding of upper management's goals and plans to stimulate problem solving, investigation, and creative thinking by your employees.
☐ Use a broad base of information sources.
☐ Know your employees well—their knowledge, skills, and values capabilities and areas for improvement.
☐ Have a clear sense of exactly how the work of training contributes to the overall work of the company.

Intervene directly in employees' performance improvement both for short-term and for long-term growth.

☐ Have a plan for including each employee in the organization's growth. Encourage and promote employee development—individualized and differentiated from the development of each other employee. Make people feel special, valued, and worth the company's investment in them.
☐ Support your actions with good performance analysis documents, like the ones suggested in this chapter.
☐ Show people that you care about individual employees.
☐ Tell people what you expect of them.

□ Give individuals accurate and frequent feedback about performance. Keep it objective, behavioral, and related to the knowledge, skills, and values of the person's job.
□ Demonstrate your belief in your own future, the future of individual employees, and the company's future.

8. Employability Checklist: 15 Ways to Learn on the Job from Work Itself

The following checklist presents key learning strategies that anyone can apply in order to learn from work. They are things anyone can do to enhance his or her own productivity as a learner. Trainers should be helping all employees to do these things as an organization of skilled learners takes shape. Remember that organizations of the future will depend on finely tuned learners; employability, above all, will require conscious and continuous development and growth of individual learners. Workers need to contribute independently as well as through others, and, because of both kinds of contributions, become leaders at what they do. This checklist will help you help individuals begin their learning journey right at their own workstation. (The following checklists in this chapter are reprinted from *How to Manage Training, 2E.* Copyright © 1998 Carolyn Nilson. Reprinted by permission of AMACOM, a division of American Management Association International, New York, NY. All rights reserved. http://www.amanet.org.)

Employability Checklist: 15 Ways to Learn on the Job from Work Itself

□ 1. *Stretch the limits of what you already know.* Play "what if" games with yourself as you focus on the tasks of your job.
□ 2. *Think process.* Stand back and observe how you actually do things, and see if the way in which you do them can be improved. Here are some starters: sorting, prioritizing, recognizing patterns, estimating, analyzing, synthesizing, translating, writing. Think in terms of "add, delete, or modify." Keep a log or a journal of "process improvements."
□ 3. *Think results, not just outcomes.* Imagine—that is, actually describe to yourself—the possibilities for all kinds of results from what you are doing. Thinking the "outcome" often limits one's probabilities to a much too direct way of thinking: a "this always comes out that way" kind of thinking ties on down to methods and procedures, the letter of the contract, adversarial

relationships, and rigidity. Think, rather, in terms of longer-range benefits to many different persons and added value to many different products and services.

☐ 4. *Don't confuse learning about something with learning something.* In your quest for greater knowledge in the work you are doing, get quickly beyond lists, definitions, and descriptions. For example, when you access your computer's help screen, pass quickly to the item you need and try it out immediately. It's the experimentation, not the accessing, that leads to deeper learning. Learning about help is not the same as being helped. Apply this analogy to other situations in which you are seeking deeper knowledge. Get off the description and into action as quickly as possible.

☐ 5. *Reflect.* Adopt a model, if you need to, in order to remember to reflect upon your thoughts and your actions. One model is the "Action/Reflection Learning" philosophy; another is the continuous improvement model of W. Edwards Deming: "Plan, Do, Check, Act." Consciously build in the time for reflection.

☐ 6. *Think of work as hierarchies of tasks.* Everyone's work has easier parts and harder parts. Know your work so well that you can accomplish the easier tasks more quickly and better by intentionally knowing when you are doing them; tackle the harder parts with assurance that they are merely a different configuration of tasks. Know what you need in order to perform all tasks well. Identifying the hierarchy of skills is a first step.

☐ 7. *Ask for help.* Know your limitations. Don't do bad work; ask for help.

☐ 8. *Engage in the disciplines of your work.* Think in terms of intrinsic motivation for work, not extrinsic motivation. Enjoy your relationship to what you do, not necessarily to some piece rate, some deadline, or some stopwatch. Each job has a certain rhythm, certain parameters and disciplines. Define these for yourself, and enjoy your engagement with them as you do your work. Intentional, engaged working usually is the most productive working.

☐ 9. *Identify and pursue gaps.* Don't be afraid to identify gaps in your information, your tools, your support, or any other input you believe you need in order to perform your job at peak capacity. Go after what you need.

☐ 10. *Be pro-active.* Speak up. Be your own advocate. Seek strategic alliances with others who value your work anywhere you can find them.

☐ 11. *Remember your memory.* Adult learners have an excellent and often untapped resource for learning from work: memory. We often forget to call up our earliest experiences with thorny situations by focusing too much on the here-and-now or the immediate future. Adults have memory for such things as patterned response, sounds, tactile memory, spatial relationship memory, preferred learning style, concepts, and problem-solving approaches that stand ready and waiting to be used again in new situations. At work, we somehow often forget to integrate our past experiences with our present challenges. Simply remembering to use your memory is an excellent way to tighten up your competence as a learner.

☐ 12. *Think equally in terms of giving and receiving.* Think in terms of passing it on—pass the torch, or whatever metaphor works for you. That is, every time you learn something or get a new insight, pass it on to someone else. Keep the learning building by getting and giving, getting and giving.

☐ 13. *Respect followership.* Forget being a hero, empress, conquistador, or lone ranger. Learn to be a good follower, not only to be a leader. Discover the intellectual rewards in followership; widen and develop your sense for skilled observation, active listening, intuition, and integration of past incomplete knowledge with what is new.

☐ 14. *Bring the whole into the parts.* Try to always remain aware of the whole—the big picture—to which your specific work is contributing.

☐ 15. *Talk out loud* when solving a problem, especially when teaching someone else.

Tools for Team Building

The three tools that follow in Box 6-2 are especially designed to help you devise and facilitate training for workplace teams.

Box 6-2. Tools for team building.

1. *Success Factors for Individual Learning Within the Team*—A checklist reminder to think first of individual employee development, then team development
2. *Team Performance Checklist*—A checklist of items and ideas to consider in how to measure the performance of the team
3. *Process Improvement*—Detailed examples of how to get team members thinking about how to make improvements in the way the team works together; useful as a team teaching tool to use in training or facilitation sessions

---

1. Success Factors for Individual Learning Within the Team

Use this checklist as a reminder to think first of the individual learner. The learning context for teams is a collection of individuals, not a classroom.

Clear Role Definition and Acceptance

☐ 1. Has a clear role been defined for this person?

☐ 2. Have you involved this person in the definition of the role?

☐ 3. Does this person understand this role? If not, what will you do to clarify his or her understanding of it?

☐ 4. Does this person accept this role?

Competency and Competency Development

☐ 5. Have you engaged in dialogue with this person regarding his or her competencies as he or she applies to the work of the team? Do you know this person's strengths and weaknesses? Does this person concur about strengths and weaknesses?

☐ 6. What specific steps can/will you take, together, to help this person acquire needed missing competencies for the work of the team, and enhance those he or she already has?

☐ 7. Have you considered competencies in at least these three areas:
—*Intellectual skills,* cognitive competencies, information-based knowledge
—*Motor skills,* "know-how," eye-hand coordination skills, demonstration and presentation skills, ability to observe ergonomic and safe work procedures
—*Emotional skills,* controlling temper, having patience, dealing with bias and gender, avoiding burnout, behaving ethically, being assertive, taking initiative

Personal Preferences

☐ 8. Have you discussed "psychological type" and "behavioral style" preferences with this person? Does this person know herself or himself well enough to be able to identify a personal preferred type or style?

☐ 9. Can you use specific examples of his or her work to illustrate your perception of this person's preferred way of approaching work?

☐ 10. Have you taken specific steps to encourage this person to recognize and value the personal preferences of other team members?

☐ 11. Do you show by your actions and by the rewards you give that you equally value persons for whom they are and for the unique contributions they can make because of their personal preferences?

☐ 12. What specific steps will you take to value diversity and use it as a strategic tool?

Individual Need for Affiliation

☐ 13. Have you adjusted your thinking about the expenditure of time in order to accommodate dialogue, brainstorming, exploration of fringes, peer training, guided self-study, just-in-time training, reflection, and other extemporaneous ways in which individuals learn from each other?

☐ 14. Have you intentionally set up opportunities—places and times—for the individuals on teams to focus on knotty problems and complex tasks?

☐ 15. What motivations have you devised to encourage collaboration?

2. Team Performance Checklist

Measurement of teams, like measurement of individual achievement, is an essential component of any systematic approach to the organizational development of teams. Training managers need to be involved in measurement of team performance in order to get the information you need for design and delivery of future training. Here are some tips:

☐ 1. Team performance depends on process "tuning." Devise some measurement form and rating scale through which you can collect data, expressed as numbers on a 7-point scale. Numbers are always easier to deal with than just words, especially on opinion items.

☐ 2. These are some of the processes that need to be measured:
- using resources
- communicating
- focusing and refocusing
- managing time
- making decisions
- solving problems
- interacting outside team

☐ 3. Getting quantitative data (as contrasted with qualitative data) is the foundation of measurement, including team measurement. These are some of the places to look for sources of quantitative data:

- better product yield
- fewer errors
- fewer quality defects
- fewer returns
- more sales
- better margins
- quicker delivery
- shorter development cycles
- fewer customer complaints
- more on-time targets met
- fewer safety infractions
- higher attendance
- more budgets met

☐ 4. Try to measure against both standards and a baseline of acceptable performance. Be realistic, and, especially if you haven't had any experience with teams, be sure to involve team members in the creation of the standards document. Most people want teams to succeed and want to succeed as individuals in teams; getting their help with the process of setting baseline standards and stretch standards by which they themselves will be measured is just plain good business.

☐ 5. Find others who have had experience with teams and make a contact with them in the name of "benchmarking." Business magazines, Web pages, and chat groups online are all good sources for individuals in other companies with experience. Don't be too idealistic at first: Go for the reality of standards and reflect this reality in your measurement instruments and procedures.

3. Process Improvement

Use the following lists as job aids to facilitate a team's understanding of process improvement, and their initiation of action to make process improvements. You can create your own lists. Just add "...ing" words to key concepts and terms. Making the action active through the use of "...ing" helps individuals to see that action is what is needed in order to make process improvements. You can also use these lists as a handout to team members during or after training, for their continuous reference on the job.

Here are some examples of how to get a team to focus on process improvement. The secret is to focus on the action word, the "...ing" word, getting the trainee to immediately begin thinking in terms of what he or she needs to do to make the process work better. For example:

Eliminating waste

Preventing delays

Consolidating sign-offs

Showing respect

Demonstrating enjoyment

Selecting colleagues

Configuring benefits

Teaching others

Getting agreement

Conducting a trial

By concentrating on the development of the "...ing" word—that is, by creating an action plan around that part of the process improvement phase—you will set yourself up to take action. In the examples below, it is tempting for team members to focus on the wrong part of the phrase, "vision," "outcomes," "dialogue," or "information." Action stops when you do this. Empowered employees take action. This exercise is a sure way to help employees move from a command-and-control old-style to a new team-based, empowered work force style. Here are some other ideas for process improvement. Add your own to the list:

Defining vision

Designing jobs

Asking questions

Creating solutions

Analyzing problems

Monitoring outcomes

Establishing dialogue

Practicing skills

Assessing risks

Disseminating information

Typical Application of Employee Development

The following case study of an environmental consulting agency suggests a situation in which employee development is indicated.

The Maturation of EarthWatch, Inc.

EARTHWATCH, an international consulting agency that specializes in environmental projects, has been in the business about 20 years. It has experienced orderly growth and currently has about 90 percent of the same staff it began with. It is a company in tune with today—service-oriented, knowledge-intensive, global, driven by technology, and feeling the demographic "middling out" and perhaps overreliance on younger temporary workers and consultants.

The organizational profile that follows resulted from a broad-based task force effort to collect information about the company's markets, the nature of the work force itself, and the present way in which training was produced.

Organizational Profile

1. Changing Market for Services
   - Customers are more knowledgeable and demanding.
   - New technologies are available for detection.
   - New technologies exist for cleanup.
   - More information is available and there is greater access to it.
   - Advances in communications are driving global networking and problem solving.
   - Political changes in Europe, Asia, Russia, South America, and the Middle East create opportunities for new alliances.
   - Activist groups function worldwide and are more sophisticated.
   - Global competition exists from both public (government) agencies and private corporations.

2. Our Work Force
   - To keep benefit numbers in line, we've relied on temporary staff; they now outnumber regular employees two to one.
   - There are 180 regular employees; 50 with advanced degrees (Ph.D., Ed.D., J.D.); 80 with masters' degrees (M.S., M.A., or M.B.A.).
   - Average experience of regular staff is 12 years.
   - Within three years 30 percent of staff will retire.

Continued on page 122

Continued from page 121

3. Characteristics of Our Current Training System
   - General dissatisfaction or only mild satisfaction with current courses and trainers—low or mediocre ratings on course relevancy.
   - Our focus is primarily on formal university-based courses and well-known trainers with national reputations.
   - There are no on-the-job training, apprenticeships, or internally created courses.
   - There has been a 10-percent increase of no-shows after the first day of most of our training programs.
   - Research and Development department has been competing with us for corporate funding, and we've come up short.
   - Project deadlines usurp training; we therefore spend all of our time "doing," with no time to acquire new skills.

Focus on the Issues

The organizational profile points up some clear employee development issues.

- *Competition.* EarthWatch now finds itself in a fast-changing field with numerous competitors. Its reputation is intact, but its work force is aging, the field itself is exploding with new information, its potential clients are becoming more aware and sophisticated, and its staffing pattern of relying on outsiders for the "new knowledge" is frightening top management. The present way of doing training simply doesn't work. R&D is encroaching on whatever extra corporate development resources there are.

- *Updated Skills.* Clearly, EarthWatch is faced with employee development issues as the intact employee base requires updated skills in technology-related topics, and management and customer service techniques. It needs current education and new knowledge regarding worldwide financial, economic, and political changes, as these changes impact environmental policy.

- *Balance Between Regular and Temporary Staff.* Obviously, EarthWatch must confront the past practice of hiring temporary employees, especially because these temporary consultants and technicians are typically the younger and more recently educated staff. Development issues need to be addressed for this population, especially if they are to become part of the regular staff. How the older regular employees transfer their knowledge to the younger employees will be an issue as the regular staff is naturally reduced by attrition over the next three years.

Employee Development as the Pivot Point for Training System Development

And finally, EarthWatch must address the design and delivery of training itself. The focus on employee development has uncovered a crying need for training system development too. Like many other small and midsize organizations, exemplifying the 1990s and positioned for growth, EarthWatch is addressing its particular development issues through training.

Chapter 7

Introducing Training

Although most people consider training an opportunity of employment, they are reluctant to commit time away from their regular jobs to participate in it. As the person in charge of training, you, naturally, have the bigger picture in mind regarding the overall benefits of training and its contributions to productivity and better business in general.

However, your employees scattered out there around the company don't share your larger perspective, and they really can't be expected to. Although training may be generally thought of as a good thing, you'll still need to plan some advertising, do some internal public relations on behalf of training, and develop a conscious sales effort for training in order to accomplish your management goals, as well as employees' individual development goals.

Training must be introduced in such a way that employees understand its benefits for both the company and themselves. They'll have to be convinced that it's to their own personal advantage to engage in training; and you'll have to understand that employees work for your company because they want to work, not because they want to go to school.

All of this means that you must be careful about how you introduce training to your employees. You can't assume that because you know it's good for them, they will think it is too. You simply have to plan, create, develop, evaluate, and modify all the information about training that you circulate among employees. Take nothing for granted; plan carefully to communicate with employees about training. An information campaign is the first step in a training marketing function that, if done correctly with good planning, can be expected to result in the changed behavior that you had in mind when you first decided that training could solve a business problem.

This information can include announcements, flyers, brochures, electronic bulletins, catalogs, schedules, and articles in newsletters, newspapers, and journals. You must also plan the introduction of outsiders—seminar leaders, to whom you have to expose your employees, and consultants, whom you have chosen to work with you and your staff on specific training problems. Communication about training is a very important, and often overlooked, management function of the person in charge of training—especially in charge of a new training operation.

Selling the Reasons for Training

First, you have to be absolutely clear in your own mind about the reasons for the training you are offering. Think primarily about the business reasons, that is, how the outcome of training will make the business better. Some of these outcomes might be:

- Better margins
- Happier customers
- More sales
- Fewer rejects
- Lower recruitment expenses
- Tighter schedules
- Fewer accidents
- Faster turnaround
- Fewer grievances
- Less litigation
- More promotions
- Fewer absences

Think in terms of results that can be measured by counting something—days, dollars, marks on a checksheet, occurrences. Make the reasons for training tangible and real; explain them in bottom-line business terms that mean something to those whom you are trying to get to sign up for training. Fit the "treatment" to the "diagnosis" as specifically as you possibly can.

Second, think in terms of the learning level of the specific individuals for whom you are planning the training and the categories of learning that you are targeting. This is where your clear thinking about the knowledge, skills, and values distinctions pays off. You should be able to communicate the educational reasons for training; that is, you must get the employee to understand that the proposed training will help him or her to gain new knowledge, acquire new skills, or get new insights about values or attitudes that are important to the job.

You'll find it a great help to your sales pitch to be able to differentiate between higher-level knowledge and skills and lower-level ones. Try to avoid pitching your promotional material at the wrong level. Don't make the mistake of promoting low-level skills for a target employee who's at a much higher level of understanding and performance. Don't attempt to attract employees to values courses that they obviously don't need if they're already doing things right. Sell the right training for the right reasons, and you'll have no problem getting people to sign up!

Getting the Timing Right and Using Channels

There are two basic timing issues when it comes to introducing training. One is the issue of planning ahead to allow enough time for the potential trainee to respond to you. The other is the issue of building expectation, and therefore motivation, through "brand identification" and consistency in your promotional products and the timing intervals of their introduction. We'll deal with each issue separately.

Keeping in mind that your intent is to cause an employee to change the way he or she does work, you'll want to be sure to work in small incremental steps to get that employee to buy into the necessity of making that change. One effective standard marketing strategy is to go for involvement of your target employee very early in the promotional effort. Retailers do this by getting buyers to clip coupons for products on sale or by mailing samples in bright packaging to buyers' homes. In training promotion, this strategy translates into allowing enough time for employees to respond to your announcement—by your suggesting what their first step must be to get "in on" whatever training opportunity you are offering to them. You should design your first promotional announcements about training so that your potential trainees have time to engage their thinking about training and take some small initial action to "cement" their interest. In later announcements, you go for commitment of a stronger sort: for example, discounts on early registration, opportunity for participation in the design of the evaluation. The trick is to plan far enough ahead that you have adequate time for the potential trainee to respond to you. Good training public relations is a system, and all good systems need feedback to drive them forward.

The basic elements in a training marketing strategy follow. They must be timed right and funneled through the most appropriate channels.

- *Recognizing the Problem.* Be sure your target trainee recognizes the business problem that training can solve. Employees are often so much in their own little worlds that they are unaware of the larger business problems. In your training public relations, you must help employees recognize the big picture before you promote the specific training that you have in mind.
- *Instilling a Comprehension of the Training Solution.* Be sure to provide information to employees so that they can connect the proposed training with the problem. They should be able to build in their own minds the beginning of a rationale for why they, themselves, might want to get involved in this training. Be sure that you give them specifics of when and where, how much and who—details of the proposed training—so that they can begin to check their calendars, consult their supervisors, and adjust their work schedules to engage in the training.
- *Personally Legitimizing the Proposed Training.* In your promotional efforts, you'll need to do something that encourages potential trainees to take a stand for training. This might be done by having a sign-up sheet in a visible location, by doing a drawing or raffle for a free place in class, by appointing a representative from key departments as a contact person, or by asking several key people to post notices around their departments for you. People have a tendency to commit themselves to something others are doing, and you'll want to take advantage of this "bandwagon" effect in getting employee participation.
- *Making Sure Trainees Show Up.* Don't assume that those who told you that they were coming will actually show up, even if the fee has been paid and their supervisors have signed a release form. Always remind yourself that most employees consider training something extra, not part of their regular work, and that you will always have to take that added step—the critical "trial" stage of marketing—to get your employee to actually show up for training.

Do some last-minute telephoning, visit the employee's workstation near the end of the day before training is set to begin, or phone the employee at home the evening before. Ask questions that can elicit a "yes" answer, such as "You know that tomorrow morning's training is due to begin at 8:30, right?" or "Our records show that you will be the only one from your department in tomorrow's CBT course. Is this correct?" Borrow the techniques that telephone marketers use on you; remember that your simple goal in this phase of introducing training is to get the employee to just show up.

Tell yourself over and over again that training must be promoted and introduced in a planned, systematic way—it will never happen just because people generally think it's a worthwhile endeavor. You have to make it happen.

- *Completing the Training and Demonstrating New Knowledge, Skills, and Attitudes.* One of the reasons why you'll often find refreshments served during training is that people need to feel comfortable and cared for during training because they have a natural tendency to feel personally exposed and somewhat at risk of failure during learning. Pleasant surroundings, food, and drink are offered to compensate for what the trainee "gives up" during the training situation. Food and drink, in this sense, can be considered as part of the conscious marketing strategy for training. Without the basic human psychological needs being met, learning will not progress.

  Your goal is to have the trainee complete the training and to demonstrate in the training context that new knowledge, skills, or attitudes have been attained. In marketing, this is the "adoption" phase, and it is the beginning of behavior change.

- *Following Up.* The final strategy you must pay attention to in terms of your training marketing is the follow-up phase after the formal lessons are done and the employee is back on the job. In marketing theory, there's a saying that "dissonance is greatest immediately after joining." This means that when you first try out a new product, your skepticism is greatest—will that new toothpaste really taste better, will my new car get me home from the dealership without problems, or can I actually do my job better by applying the new skill I just learned in training?

  What good consumer products marketers do to deal with the dissonance phenomenon is to follow up your predicted moment of "joining" by having you fill out a survey after your first usage of the toothpaste, by phoning you to be sure you got home safely with no hassles in your new car, and, often, by mass advertising through "satisfied customer" testimonials in newspapers and on radio and television in target market areas.

Trainers can adapt some of these strategies to the training dissonance situation, where the recently trained employee begins to practice what he or she learned during training. Chances are that the trainee who gets some kind of follow-up soon after training—around the probable "dissonance" time—will be more likely to continue the changed behavior, just as the consumer whose good judgment was reinforced by follow-up is more likely to continue using the toothpaste or telling others what a great car this one is!

Throughout the implementation of a training marketing strategy, timing of each activity is important. Timing is also important when you produce and circulate the various informational products of training: flyers, catalogs, posters, registration forms, newsletters, and simple announcements. You should think about the timing issue in terms of both the strategic and the product focus. This is important for online promotions too.

Here are some ideas for building "brand loyalty" through the products of training information and by creating expectation:

- Choose a special paper on which to print all training information—for example, pure white 24-pound paper, light blue light gloss paper, buff-color 20-pound paper with a coarse tooth.
- Adopt a graphic design that will become identified with training information. For example, always have a fine-line, double maroon border, always use the same type style, always print in boldface, always use three-fold announcements, always put your training department logo in the same place on each communication.
- Aim for dissemination of training information at the same time each week or month—for example, every Wednesday afternoon or on the first day of each month.
- Get public recognition for your efforts at least once every quarter through newspaper or television coverage.
- Publish a regular newsletter—for example, every other month or at the end of the month.
- Include training announcements with daily electronic bulletin board information.

- Put training opportunity posters up in a particular space in employee lounges, in hallways, and in the cafeteria and update them at regular intervals.
- Get the catalog out around the same time each year.
- Use a different color paper for each kind of training—for example, always yellow for sales training, blue for management training, green for safety training.
- Show a short training video at the beginning of every course, promoting upcoming training opportunities during the next three months.

Choosing the Best Promotional Angle

You need to think about training promotion in the same way that you think about promotion of any new consumer product or service. Personal networking, print, computers, telephone, video, and public media each have their special role. Various kinds of training information will be more appropriate for one kind of promotional medium than another. For example, last-minute reminders could be made by a personal visit, a telephone call, or an electronic mail message. Before you do that particular kind of promotion, you'll have to assess which of the three media is the most appropriate. The personal visit is probably the one with the greatest odds of delivering the result you want; the other two are progressively fraught with the risk of the person not receiving the telephone message or not taking the time to log on for electronic mail.

A "home video" produced during training could be used to show other employees how the new skills can be used and to generate enthusiasm for others to sign up for a similar course. It could be used in a variety of ways: at regular department or team meetings prior to the offering of the next similar course, in the lobby area for visitors and employees passing through to casually look at, as a course "handout" for those who took the course and learned the skills featured, and so on.

The point is that supervisors, managers, customers, former trainees, and future trainees all have the potential to become marketing channels for your training efforts. Your first step in making them work for you is to recognize that certain people, certain angles, and certain media should be tapped for the various training marketing tasks that confront you. Effective consumer marketing is seldom the same pitch to a general audience, and effective training marketing, likewise, has to be differentiated and targeted.

Advantages of Planning the Introduction of Training

The ideas in the following list might all seem very obvious, and indeed they are. They're included here because training managers often forget what they consider the obvious in their haste to get on with running the course.

- You'll find out the differences among employees by their reactions to and feedback from your information campaign.
- You'll get important input regarding individual styles and readiness levels for training from the reactions to your promotional efforts.
- You'll help employees clarify the reasons for training.
- You'll motivate employees to take advantage of existing opportunities for training and to seek future training opportunities.
- By using a variety of marketing techniques, you'll get a good idea of what works and what doesn't work. When your promotional system is broken into small parts or phases, you'll have a better chance of making corrective moves expeditiously.
- You'll never make the mistake of thinking that information equals behavior. Telling someone that training is available hardly ever results in improved work. *Marketing* training often does!

Tools for Designing Training Promotions

The six tools in this chapter, which are summarized in Box 7-1, will lead you step by step through the actual introduction and scheduling of training and the design of training promotion documents. The checklist, guidelines, and template will guide you through both the elements of choice and decision making and the actual graphics of training public relations. Although several tools are included that deal with external communications, the primary focus of these tools is on internal communication.

Box 7-1. Tools for introducing and promoting training.

1. *Checklist for the Design of Bulletins, Flyers, and Brochures*—Design considerations for each of these one-shot, timely promotional pieces

2. *Catalog Template*—A graphic representation of the major components of a training catalog, with an explanation of each block of information

3. *Scheduling Guidelines*—A list of reminders when creating your training schedules and suggestions about how to build some marketing strategies into the simple task of scheduling

4. *Rationale for Writing Articles*—A checklist for why you might want to use a story about training as a promotional device or as a way to introduce training

5. *Format Guidelines for Three Different Kinds of Publications: Newsletters, Newspapers, and Professional Journals*—The essentials you need to know when you choose to write for "the outside"

6. *Guidelines for Integrating Outsider Seminar Presenters and Consultants With Your Own Staff*—How some basic marketing techniques can make the blend work

1. Checklist for the Design of Bulletins, Flyers, and Brochures

When you're just getting training going in a growing company, you'll probably rely heavily on these three kinds of promotional pieces: bulletins, flyers, and brochures. Each is slightly different from the other, with characteristics that make it preferable over another in certain situations.

In electronically networked companies, you'll be tempted to always use electronic bulletins, but this medium might not really get the right message across. In companies that still rely heavily on paper, you'll be tempted to always write memos or send flyers around, but they might not be right for the response you want from employees. A brochure might look great, but could be overkill. These and other considerations should be foremost in your mind as you plan the introduction of training. This checklist will help focus your thinking:

Design Checklist

☐ Make an informed decision about which promotional document to use, giving careful consideration to the effect of the medium on the message.

- *Bulletins* are electronic, video, audio, or print announcements that often respond to quick changes. They are short

---

and succinct, generally addressing only the reason for the change. They generally require immediate action or response from the receiver.

Examples: changes in time or place of training, change of instructor, or cancellation of a course.

- *Flyers* are pieces of paper that describe a training event and promote the reasons why individuals might want to become involved. They are generally only one page, designed to be visually attractive, meant to be kept or posted by the employee as a reminder about the event.

  Examples: reminders that "The new open-enrollment lunchtime mini-training program is due to begin Thursday ... those interested in continuing education are welcome." "The field trip vans will leave at 7:30 a.m. from the west parking lot ... coffee, juice, and muffins will be available on board ... those who need to know more about ergonomic workstations should attend."

- *Brochures* are generally two- to four-folded papers, often of heavy-weight stock, that give a rather extensive description of a planned seminar or course. The course dates, objectives, list of topics, location, instructor's name and biographical information (and sometimes a photo), cost, and registration information are included. Brochures give you a chance to be a little "salesy."

  Example: a brochure promoting an English as a Second Language course, taught by a former Panamanian Olympic medalist, for persons for whom Spanish is their native language.

☐ Include dates and contact persons on each promotional piece. (It's easy to overlook these items in your focus on the promotional language!)

☐ Before going public, recheck the objectives for training from the learner's point of view and make sure you are satisfied that the difficulty of the learning matches the target audience for the promotional piece.

☐ Prune your mailing list so that people don't get duplicates.

2. Catalog Template

At some point during the process of introducing training in your company, you'll have enough courses to warrant having a catalog.

When this time comes, you'll want to present all courses in a similar fashion so that they each have an equal chance of being chosen by employees. Potential trainees generally "go shopping" through a catalog. You'll want to be sure to give the same kind of information about each course. Prepare a catalog template like the one shown in Figure 7-1 to be sure you include all the essentials. This goes for an online catalog or a paper catalog.

Figure 7-1. Sample catalog template for course essentials.

Catalog Template

Course number   Course title

Name of curriculum in which this course is found

Course Description

Objectives for the Trainee   **Major Topics**

- _____   - _____
- _____   - _____
- _____   - _____
- _____   - _____
- _____   - _____
- _____   - _____

Target audience _____

Prerequisites (knowledge, skills, experience, courses) _____

Instructional delivery mode (self-paced, computer-based, lecture, etc.) _____

Course length _____

Source: C. Nilson, *Training Program Workbooks & Kit*, (Paramus, NJ: Prentice Hall, 1989). Reprinted by permission of the publisher, Prentice Hall Direct A Division of ARCO.

3. Scheduling Guidelines

When you introduce training, remember that there are several kinds of schedules:

- The master schedule of courses listed for a long-range period of time—a month, three months, six months, one year
- A calendar-type monthly schedule
- A course-by-course weekly schedule of events internal to the course across the days of the week
- The daily agenda of each course set out in time blocks

Each type of schedule promotes training in its own way. These are some considerations when doing schedules:

- Use the longer-range schedules to give the most general information. This helps employees plan ahead and sparks their interest in the widest possible training opportunities.
- Specify the format of the course in the weekly schedule, for example, lab each morning, video on Wednesday afternoon, group discussion on Friday afternoon, CEO visit Monday at lunch. This helps employees relate to those aspects of the course most attuned with their own learning styles or preferences. Often it's easier for participants to accept the parts of the course they don't like when they can see ahead of time the activities they do like. The point is that you can use the schedule to motivate employees and convey the message that there's something for everyone in this course.
- Posting specific time blocks on the daily course agenda ahead of time sends the message to employees that your instructor has planned this course carefully and doesn't intend to waste the trainee's time. Remember, time on the job is how employees are compensated, and they view time as a precious commodity. You want to be sure that potential trainees understand that you run your training operation with the same concern and controls on efficiency they use on their jobs. Your careful attention to the time elements of each day of training can convey a powerful message that you understand their situation.
- Always seize the opportunity either at the beginning or the end of each course to talk about other training opportunities coming up in the near future; include a monthly (calendar-type) schedule as a handout. Specify cutoff dates for

registration of especially popular courses or programs. Remember the old marketing axiom that future customers are probably very much like present customers—your current trainees will probably tell their colleagues about training if they've had a good training experience. And if they haven't had a good experience, you'll have a chance to find out why just by doing a little public relations at the end of each course.

- Choose spaces around the company for posting master schedules and monthly schedules. Get employees used to looking for training scheduling information in the same places; build up some expectation by familiarity.
- Always have a current phone number and contact person's name on each schedule. Send the message that training is personal.

4. Rationale for writing articles

There are times when you'll want to use the promotional device of a story or article instead of the "facts only" approach of brochures, catalogs, and schedules. By putting narrative and descriptive text around the facts, you can often induce dialogue and interest about training that the more cut-and-dry forms of promotion can't.

You may choose to write an article for your company newsletter or create a new training newsletter, for these reasons:

1. You have someone on your staff who writes this kind of human interest story well.
2. You have a company culture of personal interest—employee clubs and informal social gatherings are popular; your particular employees like to know personal stories about other employees.
3. You'd like to tell employees about training in a less formal way than through the standard memos, flyers, and schedules.
4. You believe that a human interest article about past training success will generate enthusiasm, or at least dialogue, about future training.
5. You have enough lead time to write the article, take and develop pictures, and get approvals for publication in order to meet the newsletter's deadline and to still be timely regarding the training.

5. Format Guidelines for Three Different Kinds of Publications

When you write for a general audience, and often one "outside" of your target audience for training, you need to remember that readers expect to read news. This means that you have to make your writing newsworthy. Here are the guidelines for the three types of publications:

Newsletters

- Use newsletter articles to tell about training that has occurred.
- Focus on the person or persons who excelled at the specific training you are promoting.
- Get their names spelled correctly, their job titles correct, and their department or group titles correct.
- Give the featured person's boss some credit, especially if he or she paid for the employee to take the course.
- Tell about the results of training—the use of new skills, or how the training improved sales, profit, attendance, safety, or whatever.
- Include your name and phone number so that readers who want more information about this featured course or any other course will know whom to contact.

Newspapers

- Organize your information around the Five Ws: Who, What, When, Where, Why. Make up an outline under each W category.
- Know exactly who you want to talk to at the newspaper office: the editor, a friend, or a specific reporter. Never submit a press release blind. Do your networking and your homework first. It's a people business.
- Have a newsworthy slant—what changed, why it's important, what well-known names are associated with this, which local towns do they come from, etc.
- How will this training news affect the people who buy newspapers? Be sure that you know the answer to this question before you try to convince a newspaper staffer to listen to your story.
- If you want to promote training through public means (including radio and TV news), be sure that your training story touches a current concern of the medium you've tar-

geted—for example, the environment, adult literacy, hazardous waste, VDT safety, day care, paternity leave, etc.

Professional journals

- Read the journal you've targeted very carefully to study its style and the slant of most of the articles. Be prepared to write your article in the same style and with a similar slant, or abandon the project.
- Study the format (for example, indents, spacing after headings, level of headings, length) before you begin writing your article.
- Be absolutely sure you can stick to the journal's preferred order of presentation: abstract first, overview or literature review next, methodology next, etc.
- Do the tables and figures in proper format.
- Follow this journal's style of footnotes and bibliography.
- Know how this journal treats results and conclusions. Be sure that you understand how they prefer to conclude an article.
- Be sure that your article will still be timely and relevant to the journal's readership by the time it finally gets published. Don't submit an article that will soon become dated. Choose a subject that is newsworthy from a future point of view—one whose results have implications for further investigation or that can be replicated by others in a situation similar to yours.
- Get a copy of the journal's guidelines for reviewers before you begin to write. Some of the factors reviewers might consider are: current importance of the topic to the field in general, quality of the literature review, choice of statistics or evaluation methods, the specificity of conclusions, the strength of analysis, etc.
- You'll be rated on both form and substance—be ready for both!
- Clarify your own motivations for wanting to write a journal article before you begin. Be sure that the audience for the journal is important enough to your training operation for you to go through the process. Getting published in journals can send messages that your operation is "leading edge," and this might be very helpful as your business grows.

6. Guidelines for Integrating Outsider Seminar Presenters and Consultants with Your Own Staff

Employees and their supervisors these days are very concerned about quality issues—how to build in quality standards and how to measure whether or not quality is resulting in both products and services. Concerns about quality are often expressed by your staff when it comes to relying on outsiders to design or deliver training for you. After all, the outsiders don't know exactly how you operate, and it's hard for them to quickly learn to accept and adopt your company's values. You can do a lot to ward off questions about your vendor's or consultant's quality by carefully introducing this person to your staff. These are some general guidelines:

- Focus on the personal characteristics and elements of experience that are precisely in tune with what your trainees base their values on. Stress, for example, the vendor's experience teaching the same course in another company that your company holds in esteem, a professional association of the consultant with a key person in your company (service on the same board of directors), or the ways in which the objectives of this vendor's seminar specifically address the concerns raised by your staff during program evaluation last quarter.

- Create a consultant monitoring plan or project plan with key members of your company so that the insiders get a real chance to be in control of the work of the consultant. Insist that the consultant develop a working arrangement with your staff before the work begins.

- Appoint a project manager or single contact person from your staff to manage the work of the consultant. Be sure that finances and communications are crystal clear and that plans for both are agreed upon by your project manager and the outside service provider.

- Be sure that your staff and the outsider know what the expected products or outcomes of the training services will be. Assess and evaluate the work being done against the agreed-upon plan to work toward these "deliverables."

- Do everything you can think of in terms of communications to prevent politicking and pointing fingers—you want the outsiders to complement your staff, not cause divisions in it.

- Stick to your plan for collaboration with the outsider, document activities, and adjust your plan if it's not working. Remember to implement the feedback and corrections loop of any good communication system!

The Toughest Training Task: Targeting the Top—Language Improvement for Managers and Technical Professionals

This case study illustrates many principles of good communication around the introduction of training. The training manager had the particularly difficult job of introducing a new course of a somewhat sensitive nature to the toughest target audience—highly educated, high-level managers and technical professionals. Not surprisingly, the successful introduction of this course was handled by a manager whose title is "Manager, Training and Communications." Her intuitive and well-planned information actions before training ever began contributed in great measure to the success of the training that eventually was designed and presented to her growing and changing R&D company.

Here's what happened:

Introducing English as a Second Language at Aeronautical Radio, Inc., and ARINC Research Corp.

The ARINC companies, with headquarters near Washington, DC, provide advanced communications, information services, and management and engineering expertise to the airlines and the U.S. government. They employ engineers, software experts, systems specialists, a variety of technical managers, and other R&D scientists and technical specialists. A growing number of ARINC's high-level professionals are foreign-born and speak English as their second, that is, non-native, language. ARINC's training manager believed that the company could benefit from training that helped these employees write, read, and speak better English, and she found a consultant who could custom-design the training.

Most of the potential target audience for this training had in fact studied English in their own countries, excelled as technical students, and were functioning as competent workers in responsible jobs at ARINC where American English is the norm. Convincing such high-performing, highly driven, and high-level

Continued on page 142

Continued from page 141

employees to set aside time for language study was no small task. Getting these managers to agree that project deadlines, testing schedules, and the intensity of client-based R&D work could give way to reading and writing—and getting the individuals themselves to commit that they needed the training—were somewhat formidable communication challenges. Getting ARINC's internal technical writing instructors and documentation specialists to accept an outside consultant was also a communication challenge that had to be met before the dialogue on training development issues could even begin. Introducing this particular training required skillful management.

These are some of the key communications strategies used by the training manager:

1. She "sold" the business reasons for better English.
    - It would improve quality of customer contact.
    - There would be better presentations and less meeting time.
    - There would be more visibility and opportunity for foreign-born professionals, consistent with ARINC's worldwide client base and future direction.
2. She pitched the level and focus properly.
    - Training would cover a variety of language skills.
    - The approach would be very analytical.
    - Classes would be small and highly individualized.
    - The instructor and peers would give supportive feedback in a protected setting.
3. She developed her channels.
    - She sought input to confirm the need for the training from the manager of the technical writing group, the primary instructor of the technical writing course, and the internal training coordinator for engineering training.
    - She sent memos and electronic mail to managers of project managers and other managers whose work would be made easier by having reports come to them in better form and with correct usage of standard American business English.
    - She used third-party "testimonials" in the form of written commendations and newspaper articles about the consultant's work in other companies to reinforce her decision to go outside for this training.
4. She allowed enough lead time.
    - She started the process in January.

- By the end of March, the consultant and several key "channel" persons had shared information and ideas, and training design documents were circulated among selected ARINC staff.
- In April, she clarified the internal accounting necessary to fund the course, and she set the dates for training.
- In May, the custom course was developed.
- In June, she got commitments from the trainees.
- In July, the course was delivered.

5. She provided an assistant on the first day of training to be available to make phone calls if trainees didn't show up.
   - The assistant confirmed the trainee list ahead of time.
   - The assistant was present on the first day of training to welcome trainees and verify that all materials and the training room were in order.

6. She got people to show up and to complete the training. Training was delivered as planned; class exercises and comments on evaluation forms demonstrated that learning had indeed occurred. Typical titles of those who took the course were: manager of data communications, quality manager, senior principal software engineer, researcher in analog simulation, advanced strategic technical planning engineer, director of satellite communications, and staff analyst in quality management.

7. She followed up after training, addressing the "dissonance is greatest after joining" issue in marketing. In August, she reported that she had received notice from several managers saying that they "hoped she would set up this training again," thus completing the marketing cycle—including verifying that she had satisfied customers! And, in fact, about six months later, the course ran again with a similar target audience and with similar success.

Focus on the Issues

This case is presented in this level of detail to illustrate the essential point made throughout this chapter that *introducing* training is just as important as designing and delivering it. ARINC's training manager is a master at communication. Her implementation of a marketing strategy is the foundation for training that works. The two basic issues illustrated by this case are that:

1. *Training must be introduced* according to principles of good marketing and communication.
2. *Linking the training information system with the instructional design system* can lead to more effective—and more—training services.

Training as a Solution to Problems

Psychologically, training comes at the end of an analysis process. Generally, some problem has surfaced before training is considered as the human resources intervention of choice. Training often starts out in what could be considered a negative context, which makes it all the more important to have a carefully planned and executed information campaign. The best way for you to think about the training you propose is to think of it as a solution to a very specifically identified problem or set of problems.

In addition, training is generally viewed by everyone concerned as not being part of a person's job; seldom does one earn bonuses or recognition for taking courses; seldom can one charge an operational account for time spent in class. Moreover, often training costs are stated in terms of time spent away from the job. Your best way to compensate for this typical mind-set is to develop training objectives that enable individuals to do their jobs better and more easily and to have a promotional plan that keeps the business value of training foremost in employees' minds, top drawers, e-mails, and office walls!

Training that "sticks" is a people business, a learning endeavor, and a marketing enterprise.

Chapter 8

Analyzing Needs and Designing Training

This chapter gives you helpful ideas and practical guidelines for looking at a course or training program with the confidence to know that its design will lead to new knowledge or skills. This chapter helps you sort out the advertising hype from the educational psychology and develop a set of standards against which to evaluate the design of training.

Whether you write your own courses, buy them already made, or hire a consultant to write them for you, this chapter clarifies the meaning of good instructional design and explains how the "technology" of instructional systems design can work for you. Whether you choose to purchase training or do it yourself, this chapter helps you do it better.

Training Design and the Quality Connection

One of the basic principles of all quality systems and methodologies is that building quality "into" your endeavor will pay off in the end. This means that instead of waiting until the end of a product line to do an inspection, those in charge of that product in each step of its development should inspect the product as they complete their small part. In procedures and processes of work, "building in quality" means that each step along the way is validated and checked for accuracy and usefulness to the procedure or the process as a whole.

By looking for errors *as development occurs,* one can much more easily find the errors and correct them. Looking for better ways of dealing with raw materials, inventories, shipping, schedules, steps, logic, procedures, and a host of other tangible and identifiable parts of products and processes will, according to all the quality gurus, in the long run result in more and better outcomes. "Quality of products and services" is one of the Malcolm Baldrige Quality Prize categories. A 1991 article in *Training & Development* discusses W. Edwards Deming, who addresses the "building quality in" issue and lists several caveats, including: cease dependency on mass inspection to achieve quality; improve constantly the system of production and service; and put everyone in the company to work to accomplish the transformation.

Training is a business function that has both products and processes as outcomes. There are courses, manuals, videotapes, CBT programs, slides, transparencies, job aids, tests, laboratory sessions; there are also processes such as generating a table of contents for courses, listing objectives for the learners, developing practice exercises and tests, and designing evaluations of learning. Well-designed training builds quality into each product and each process associated with each course or training event. By designing your own courses, you can more conveniently "build in quality" during the design processes and as each product of design is completed. It's harder to ensure that quality has been built in to a course that someone else has developed or that you buy out of a catalog.

In the world of training design, "doing it right the first time" means that an appropriate range of expert opinion has been consulted in order that a valid, necessary, and sufficient content outline can be written. It also means that customers and potential trainees have been asked to contribute their ideas and expectations regarding the results of training—before the objectives get written. It means that criterion measures have been established with input from those who will depend upon the trained employee to apply what he or she has learned. It means that training experiences and lessons have been designed to be delivered in ways that fit what is being learned and match what the trainee is expected to do back on the job after having been trained. It means that you know what has to be done during the various phases of training design and development in order for training to be "right the first time."

In training, you often don't get another chance. Employees who have given up their production schedules to be trained will not take kindly to a poor course. They will not schedule other training voluntarily, and they will not hesitate to criticize you in writing at the end of training. They will tell others to avoid that particular training, and they probably will not take another course from you. Supervisors who have spent their budgets for employees to attend seminars and classes will expect to get their money's worth in terms of greater productivity from employees who have gone through training. Training should be right the first time; this is the challenge and responsibility of the instructional designer—and that's the quality link.

The Top 10 Guidelines for "Building in Quality" During Training Design

The following guidelines will help you if you've chosen to write your own courses. They will also be useful when you get around to revising courses, and they can help you evaluate courses written by a vendor or consultant. The guidelines are based on the notion that training design is one phase in an instructional system; that it requires inputs to validate its structure; and that it has outputs that can be evaluated against rigorous design criteria.

1. *Spend a lot of time identifying the target audience for this particular training.* Check with at least three sources. Your goal is to design training as specific as possible to the job requirements of these particular trainees.

2. *Think of these trainees as customers, and know what they expect regarding quality.* Do they expect practice exercises built into the course? Do they expect high-level courses focused on problem solving and making judgments? Do they expect high-quality binding of their course manuals? Do they expect an extensive bibliography? Do they expect the big name instructor even if it means waiting several months until he or she is available? Your customer's quality expectations will affect the way in which you design your training. Don't be too quick to jump to conclusions or make assumptions. High quality could mean that your course should focus on low-level skills, coaching support, more than normal amounts of feedback, disposable worksheets, job aids to take home, or some other process or product standard that might never have occurred to you as being important. Seek advice from your customers and listen to them.

3. *Break design and development processes into activities with beginnings and ends.* Identify the product that will result from each process. For example, an outline of three levels will result from discussions about the scope and sequence of the content of training; a five-minute practice test will result from design deliberations on trainee evaluation at the end of module six. Set achievable design goals.

4. *Hold a design review of each product.* For example, check the content outline of the course or the lists of objectives or the group of lab sessions, as each product is completed. Monitor your own work and each other's work. Think of design reviews as team efforts, and involve all significant parties as review team members.

5. *Identify errors and count them.* Only by careful scrutiny and hard work against standards will you be able to find and correct errors in design work. When you do find errors, correct them right away while the design thinking is fresh in the minds of the designers. This in-process evaluation and correction saves enormous amounts of time in the long run. And you'll be absolutely amazed at how the next course you design has fewer errors, and the next course, even fewer errors. Think of errors as your friends—they help you build in quality.

6. *Build broad ownership of the course.* During the design phase involve your peers (other subject matter experts from else-where in the company, other managers, potential customers) in validating the design or as members of product review teams. Don't design training in isolation—it's not *your* course, it's *theirs.*

7. *Define objectives for the learners, not the presenters.* When creating objectives, think small—what the learner can accomplish in about 15 minutes time. Think about the ways in which you'll be able to tell whether or not the learner has gotten the point of the training. During design, think mostly about how to organize and "pitch" the instruction so that these particular trainees can learn quickly. Only by thinking in small segments can you ever hope to design training that can be learned. "Lofty" thinking will get you into trouble during design. Keep it simple, teachable, measurable, and learnable.

8. *Remember the business reasons why you are writing this course.* Design in the opportunity for transfer of learned skills to the trainee's job. Do this in as many places in the course as you possibly can. Just-in-time training is a concept worth pursuing. Keep training practical; shy away from the theoretical. "Need to know" is the watchword, not "nice to know."

9. *Let people know that this course is tied to the life and breath of your company.* During the entire design process—specifying the target audience, figuring out the content, establishing objectives for the learner, creating exercises and tests of achievement, setting course evaluation criteria, selecting media, deciding on the format for manuals and handouts, conducting design reviews, doing dry runs and pilot tests—communicate to others around the company about the various design activities.

10. *Ask for feedback during design activities and use it immediately.* Report back to the feedback giver. Show people that training design is an active process, representative of broad expertise

and interest, and a process capable of renewal. Building in quality is an egalitarian principle that depends upon the *use* of feedback as a foundation.

Designs to Manage Diversity

Training for the changing American work force must be designed with the realities that as the year 2000 approaches, diversity is a greater fact of life than it ever has been in the past, and that the old American metaphor of the "melting pot" has been replaced by the "salad bowl." Like the other human resources systems, training must be designed not to assimilate and melt into oneness but to see and savor the fresh and colorful variety of differences.

Good training design has a lot going for it already in terms of its ability to value differences and, yes, even to play a big role in a company's ability to manage this diversity of the work force. Well-designed training builds in these considerations.

- Content is presented in a variety of ways to appeal to various learning styles—for example, visual learners, analytical learners, slow learners, procedure-oriented learners, creative learners, learners who love to work in pairs, solo learners, and so on.
- Objectives are tied to business goals to which all kinds of employees can relate.
- Learning experiences are designed as problems to be solved in the best way possible; a genuine respect for generating solution options from all sources is built into the design of training.
- Learning is designed around universal principles of cognitive development, with culture-free bases for presenting information so that simple skills are mastered before more advanced skills are introduced.
- Adult learning is designed with supports, feedback, facilitation, self-monitoring, formative evaluation, and corrective action. It is based on the recognition that adults are competent and deficient in skills unequally and that all are able to contribute to and manage their own learning in their own ways.

Training is uniquely poised to facilitate managing the wonderful diverse work force of the new century. Good instructional design will help to strengthen America's human capital. Its potential should never be underestimated.

The Basic Building Blocks of Instructional Design

In the next several pages, some basic building blocks of instructional design are discussed in a general way meant to introduce you to these concepts and tools. If you embark on your own training design effort, you'll need to read more in depth about learning design, building educational taxonomies, developing curriculum, and designing tests. The basic building blocks presented here are simply an introduction to the approaches of instructional design.

First, a reminder that in the systems view of training, design is but one component of a cycle. As you see from the model in Figure 8-1, it is preceded by the analysis component and followed by development, delivery or implementation, and evaluation. The systems view consistently features inputs, outputs, feedback, and modification and sets standards and measurements for these components.

Figure 8-1. Design as a component of the instruction cycle.

The Instructional System Design (ISD) Model

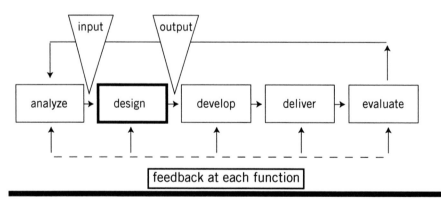

The ISD model in Figure 8-1 shows that the quality of the design very much depends on the quality of the up-front research and analysis of needs, which function as input to the design phase. In addition, the output of the design phase—the objectives, the content outline, the exercises, the media preferences—very much affect the development of the finished course. In the development phase, the content outline is fleshed out in narrative text, descriptive and explanatory comments, procedures, glossaries, and so on. Here exercises are merged into the content in the appropriate places and media are designed by graphic artists. After printing, binding, and packaging, the course is pilot tested, evaluated, and revised. Quality in development very much depends on quality output of the design phase. And so the system continues.

The point of the systems approach is that standards and measurements can be assigned to the products or outputs of each phase of training. By constantly working toward standards, taking measurements, and making modifications to processes and products throughout the system, you build quality into the finished training.

Job Analysis

One of the most essential tools for the training designer is job analysis. Remember the caution not to throw training at every human resources problem that surfaces—save training as the solution to performance problems that are based on skill and knowledge deficiencies.

Because adults are so varied in their work experience levels and in personal characteristics such as energy, health, responsibilities at home, educational background, and so on, employees do in fact have deficiencies or gaps in their understanding and abilities. The nature of adult learning is that it can hardly ever be aimed at an "average." Mass produced courses can generally be expected to produce poor results because they seldom are individual enough to efficiently and effectively meet the employee's needs.

In order to target training where it needs to be focused, you'll need to analyze the skill and knowledge requirements of each person's job so that you can find out exactly where trainees need help. To do this, it's okay to start with a person's job description, but you then have to move quickly into the realm of skills and knowledge requirements. Job descriptions usually tell the areas of responsibility, which is only part of the story. In order to find out what trainees really need to know and to not waste time in unnecessary training, you'll want to come up with a list of required skills for each of the responsibility areas and a checklist for trainees to use to tell you which skills they need help with. You can then take the next steps to design a course *customized* for your *customer.*

Another useful tool in job analysis is the "people-data-things" analysis whereby job skills are categorized into lists. Skills are identified as people skills, data skills, or things skills. Often discrepant performance occurs when there is a mismatch between the employee's expectation that a job entails dealing mostly with people, when, in fact, as the job developed, it turned into a job that deals mostly with data. In such a case, improved performance happens when either the job changes to align with the employee's expectation, or the employee is trained in how to do the data aspects of the job. Classifying skills into people-data-things categories can help you design the right kind of training for the job that needs to be done. Good training design is always a combination of design for specific people with specific needs to learn in specific jobs.

Priorities, Hierarchies, and Taxonomies

If you are designing a training package to be used with a number of trainees, you might want to develop a trainee "need to know" chart of skill. Across one axis are the skills; the other axis contains the names of trainees. By placing check marks in the cells of the chart, you get a quick idea of which are the priority skills the design of the training must address. Through your chart, you'll know, for example, that six out of 10 employees need to know how to merge computer files and import and export them within the system or that two employees require back safety training. Your need to know chart will lead you into course design.

Courses are generally designed with the "unfolding" approach: that is, the points become obvious as the training unfolds and builds upon itself. This generally means that new concepts are defined and described first; they're then explained; examples and options are given to broaden the trainee's perspective; and then analogies and problem situations are presented to engage the learner and facilitate his or her success in learning. Experienced instructional designers can also design courses that work backwards from solutions to problem definitions. They can present course content in messy chunks of information and in a variety of skill challenges to encourage intuitive and creative analysis and solution finding. Instruction can be designed by experienced designers to create learning challenges entirely through simulations, games, role plays, and case studies. The possibilities for interesting instructional design are numerous, but none will work unless the inputs to the design process are accurate, legitimate, worthy, valued by the culture, and built upon skill and knowledge needs of real employees.

Listing, prioritizing, and choosing wisely are elements of process quality that instructional designers engage in when they work with taxonomies. The two most common taxonomies that instructional designers use are cognitive skills and psychomotor skills (eye-hand coordination, small and large muscle application). The taxonomy of cognitive skills was created and codified by Benjamin Bloom in the 1950s at the University of Chicago (see the bibliography at the end of the book). His disciples soon followed with the codification of psychomotor skills. These two taxonomies have survived exhaustive analysis and experimentation over the years in educational psychology studies, and they remain strongly in use by instructional designers today.

A taxonomy is simply a classification scheme. It usually places items within the categories in a hierarchical fashion. In learning taxonomies, this means that lower-level skills or basic skills have to be learned before more advanced skills can be attempted and learned. Instructional designers make mistakes when they jump to the higher-level skills before trainees have been able to master the basics. When you evaluate someone else's course design, look for this "leveling" evidence: you want to be sure that the course in fact gives trainees a chance to learn and master lower-level skills before they go forward through the course. You'll want to be sure that the progression toward learning is appropriate, that not too much time is spent on low-level skills if the objectives clearly intend for the trainee to be at higher skill levels.

Examples of a progression of cognitive skills

- You must *define* something before you can *illustrate* its use.
- You must *list* all options before you can *prioritize* them.
- You must *recall* before you can *summarize.*
- You must *recognize* words before you can *translate* them.

Examples of a progression of psychomotor skills

- *Connect* before you *build.*
- *Stand* before you *bend.*
- *Align* before you *draw.*
- *Listen* for the beep before you *activate* the motor.

The point of showing you these examples is so that you see how easy it is to fall into the trap of designing learning backwards—or of not designing learning at all. It's all too tempting to want to jump to the outcome you expect (illustrate, prioritize, summarize, translate; build, bend, draw, activate) without allowing the learner to learn the prerequisite skills. Thinking in terms of learning taxonomies will help you design for learning. Objectives for learners must be tied to the progressive levels of skills that they need to master.

Of course there are other hierarchies and taxonomies in any typical company. These are the personal skills and organizational skills that come to be valued in a company. They include things like being on time, taking initiative, supporting those who work to improve quality, being accessible, being friendly, and so on. They might include things like following rules, working collaboratively, using feedback, and mentoring. As a training designer, you'd do yourself a big favor to find out from as many sources as possible what they think these taxonomies are and how you might go about designing those human relations and organizational development skills into your courses, too. Clarity about which "people skills" are valued in your company can have handsome payoffs as you use training to help your diverse work force contribute its best to your company.

Modules, Units, Lessons, and Objectives

These sometimes confusing terms used in instructional design deserve some clarification. Together, they form the logical divisions of a course. They are presented here in descending order of largest to smallest. Tools for creating objectives and lessons are discussed later in this chapter.

- *Module*—A set of lessons that can be readily learned together in some block of time such as a day, a half-day, an evening, a set of frames in a CBT course, or a set of workbooks in a correspondence course. In sales training, for example, you might have a module on "Various Ways to Close," "Twenty Lessons in Prospecting," or "How to Turn the Account Over to Customer Service Reps."

- *Unit*—A group of lessons that are dependent upon each other in order for learning to happen. A unit is carefully constructed out of the mass of content of a course; it has a name; it is an organized set of concepts and exercises that are meant to serve an educational purpose. A unit has an obvious developmental design, geared to lead the learner through the content. In a course on desktop publishing, a unit called "Creating Graphs" might look like this: a group of lessons on figuring out what to assign to the x axis and the y axis, a group of lessons on how to create 10 different kinds of graphs, a group of lessons on how to size your graph and place it into text. This unit might be part of a module on "Graphic Theory and Techniques in Desktop Publishing."

- *Lesson*—The learning that can be accomplished in a short period of time, for example in 15 minutes. A lesson has a very specific purpose; it is based on a small amount of content; it often contains procedures, definitions, and practice time. Every lesson should build in a few minutes of feedback from the trainer to the trainee. A lesson is governed by one or two objectives for learning that should be obvious to the trainee and which the trainee can demonstrate that he or she has mastered. Lessons have beginnings and ends, and transitions between them. Instructional designers pay a lot of attention to the scope of each lesson, the level of objectives for each lesson, and the placement of lessons within the context of each unit.

- *Objective*—A small and specific goal for learning that governs the actions of the trainee and the trainer during a lesson. A good objective tells what the learner will do in order to learn. It generally has three parts: do this, to this, and in this amount. Objectives are often related to a specific skills analysis and based on specific tasks required on the job. In training for data entry operators, an example of an objective is: *Access—the Employment History Screen of the Personnel Data System—within 30 seconds of log on.* The three parts of this objective are divided by dashes. A good objective uses an active verb; deals with very specific and recognizable items or concepts; can be taught, learned, demonstrated, and measured. One to three objectives generally govern a lesson.

A Word or Two About Evaluation

Evaluation is a process the function of which is to aid in making decisions. Therefore, no matter when you do it, on what or on whom you focus, the essential things to strive for are (1) clarity about the decision you are making and (2) importance of the data you get from the process of evaluation. Measurement of results, testing of individuals, and audits of programs have no place in training unless you evaluate for a clear reason that will contribute to business goals and the information you get will be useful in making improvements to products, services, and processes at work.

Never do evaluation haphazardly or half-heartedly. For example, the "smiles test" type of course evaluation form at the end of a

---

course is a waste of time if you don't make course improvements based on the trainees' comments. Testing a trainee just so that you have a score does no good, unless you give that trainee some feedback and corrective instruction that takes that person by another learning path to mastery of the content or skill. Know what you're about and why you need evaluation results. And remember, all training, including the evaluation piece, is based on the systems concept of input, output, and feedback.

When evaluation is used for the right reasons, that is, to accomplish business goals, it becomes a major input resource to the analysis phase of the instructional system. It is the outputs of the many processes of evaluation that have the greatest potential for facilitating improvement in business products, services, procedures, and relationships.

Advantages of Using the ISD Model for Design of Training

The focus of this chapter has been that the internal design of training—the way a course or learning event hangs together—is a critical element in ensuring training's success as a business endeavor. By following the ISD model for design of training, you can be sure that the internal structure of training will solidly relate to all of the factors that increase your likelihood of ultimately presenting successful training. These are the advantages of using the ISD model for design of training:

- Good design follows good learner needs assessment.
- You approach design itself as a unique process with its own standards and controls.
- Design efforts are systematic, with identifiable inputs and outputs and with a system mandate to ask for, receive, and use feedback on design efforts.
- Good design standards enable training developers to "get it right the first time" by correcting errors during the process of design so that training for customers is right the first time.
- Good design leads learners efficiently through content.
- Good design makes it easier for instructors to teach.
- Good design gets learners to intended outcomes of training sooner.
- Good design helps employees transfer what they learned during training to their jobs.

Tools for Designing Training

The seven tools discussed in this section (summarized in Box 8-1) are meant to provide the most basic foundation for instructional design. The subject of instructional design is the topic of full-year courses and multiyear graduate programs, so, obviously, these tools just scratch the surface—and perhaps whet your appetite for more information. They suggest the parameters of good design and provide you with the confidence you need to make useful decisions about instructional design.

Box 8-1. Tools for designing training.

1. *Six Challenges for Workforce 2000*—A brief description of the Hudson Institute's six policy challenges for American workers and the places they work during the decade 1990-2000
2. *Training Development Timeline*—A guide to managing the design process leading to the production of a new course
3. *Structuring Training So That Learning Happens*—Guidelines for designing training so that people learn, and not just take up space in class
4. *Dealing with Various Learning Styles*—Guidelines for designing training to appeal to the various styles you are likely to find among adult learners
5. *Design Standards for Various Parts of a Course*—A general listing of typical standards for objectives, content, the course setting, the instructor's delivery, training materials, instructional media, and CBT lessons
6. *Lesson Plan Format*—What to include in a lesson
7. *Worksheet for Writing Objectives*—A worksheet set up to help you list the objectives for an entire unit of instruction

---

1. Six Challenges for Workforce 2000

The Hudson Institute in its report, *Workforce 2000* (1987, pp. 105-106), summarizes the six challenges that will require rethinking and revision between now and the year 2000. Of these six challenges, five have immediate implications for instructional design. Only the first item is more likely not to have a direct challenge for designers, because it concerns change as it affects policy deliberations more than as it affects design deliberations.

- *Stimulating Balanced World Growth.* The U.S. must pay less attention to its share of world trade and more to the growth of the economies of the other nations of the world, including those nations in Europe, Latin America, and Asia with whom the U.S. competes.

- *Accelerating Productivity Increases in Service Industries.* Prosperity will depend much more on how fast output per worker increases in health care, education, retailing, government, and other services, than on gains in manufacturing.
- *Maintaining the Dynamism of an Aging Work Force.* As the average age of American workers climbs toward 40, the nation must ensure that its work force does not lose its adaptability and willingness to learn.
- *Reconciling the Conflicting Needs of Women, Work, and Families:* Despite the huge increases in the numbers of women in the work force, many of the policies and institutions that cover pay, fringe benefits, time away from work, pensions, welfare, and other issues have not yet been adjusted to the new realities.
- *Integrating Black and Hispanic Workers Fully Into the Economy:* The shrinking numbers of young people, the rapid pace of industrial change, and the rising skill requirements of the emerging economy make the task of fully utilizing minority workers particularly urgent between now and 2000.
- *Improving the Education and Skills of All Workers:* Human capital—knowledge, skills, organization, and leadership—is the key to economic growth and competitiveness.

The Hudson Institute's sequel publication to *Workforce 2000, Workforce 2020,* was published in 1997. In the new book, the same themes are echoed with an additional warning that the wage gap between rich and poor will widen and qualified workers will be found around the world. The Institute sounded an alarm about immigration policies as they affect hiring and training, and, in fact, as this book goes to press, the U.S. government has been struggling with the issue of increasing the number of work visas to accommodate the rising need for high-end workers, particularly in America's high-tech industries. The 1997 report also sounds an alarm regarding America's elementary and secondary education system, which is preparing students poorly for the workplace of jobs that require problem-solving skills, excellent language and communication skills, and advanced math. Recruitment and retainment of workers were two themes in the *Workforce 2020* study. The study points out that many of America's new jobs being created require high-skill/high-education levels, and that our worker pool is increasingly less well prepared to move into these jobs.

Instructional designers would be well-advised to begin planning to meet these five design challenges through training.

---

2. Training Development Timeline

The following timeline is included so that you can see instructional design as a developmental process that has parts, parameters, and quality guidelines. Each item in the timeline has process constraints such as timing, consensus-building, collaboration, and verification. You can work to make each of these constraints better—trimming time away from meetings, focusing on tasks more effectively, choosing collaborators more carefully, giving information to those who need it, and establishing and publicizing standards. It's controls on these kinds of processes that help to build quality into the finished products of training.

[Add date]

1. Verify content with subject matter experts _____
2. Achieve consensus among all significant parties on learning _____
   objectives
3. Achieve consensus among all significant parties on best mode _____
   of delivering this course: video, CBT, classroom, hands-on workshop
4. Verify content scope and sequence of topics with customer _____
5. Check course visual aids for clarity, accuracy, consistency, _____
   completeness
6. Set production schedule, with commitment from related _____
   organizations: customers, advertisers, graphic artists, programmers,
   instructional designers, writers, instructors, printers, registrars
7. Label and number the course; be sure that it gets into the catalog _____
8. Promote the course through all appropriate channels _____

3. Structuring Training So That Learning Happens

These guidelines are predicated on the experience of adult educators and trainers who have noted that adults learn best by connecting new information to what they already know. The learning readiness of adults depends upon the quantity and quality of their individual stores of experience. It's for this reason that we structure training in learning hierarchies and design lessons based on taxonomies of skills. The aim of well-structured training is to enable the employee to quickly and completely transfer what was learned in the protected environment of training to the job. These guidelines will help you with this structuring:

1. Structure learning objectives according to a well-ordered plan, such as lowest or easiest to highest or most difficult.
2. Analyze what you intend to teach for its intellectual (cognitive) skill components as well as its hands-on (psychomotor) skill

components. Each group of skills can be organized from easy to difficult. Present the easier ones first.

3. Consider the trainees' comfort levels during the training experience. Realize that each person has a psychological need to be protected, safe, at ease, and valued during learning. Most adults feel exposed during training; therefore, designers must design into their courses the means to meet these kinds of psychological needs. This is done by timing; opportunities for trainees to take leadership during lessons; exercises in which trainees share their knowledge with others; feedback from trainees to the instructor; practice exercises and corrective evaluation at many points during lessons; and the ordering and sequencing of course content so that it always has some elements of relationship to trainees' jobs or past experience.

4. Recognize that each trainee will have a different priority regarding the application of the training. Some trainees will need to use the new skill tomorrow, whereas others will not need to use it until next month. In other words, there is always a hierarchy of urgency. Trainees can generally be expected to learn more efficiently when the pressure to use the new learning is more immediate. This, of course, has implications for those in the class who don't have the pressure of immediacy. It can be a good idea in such situations to design the course with job aid handouts, and not just a trainee manual, so that a visible reminder of the new information can be always at hand at the trainee's work site, whether it's tomorrow or next month that it has to be used.

5. Describe before explaining; define the rules before telling why to use them; verify that new concepts have been learned before asking trainees to use them to evaluate a situation.

6. Design for the very early stages of learning. Recognize that trainees will respond differently to various visual and auditory stimuli. Build in time and options in learning at the beginning stages. Mentally focusing on the tasks at hand takes time, and there should be opportunity for expression of individual differences even in the first two or three minutes of lessons. Never jump right into the tough issues or unfamiliar content.

7. Realize that a good memory doesn't automatically happen. Enhancing one's memory depends upon mastering a hierarchy of skills designed to do just that. In designing training to help trainees remember, strive for consistency in the way you express yourself, be sure that the procedures you write are complete and

in fact follow one another as stated (try them out), write in mnemonic devices, provide cues, suggest analogies, point out relationships, provide guided practice. These guidelines and the ones in the following section are adapted from a previous work of the author. (Reprinted from *How to Manage Training, 2/E.* Copyright © 1998 Carolyn Nilson. Reprinted by permission of AMACOM, a division of American Management Association International, New York, NY. All rights reserved. http://www.amanet.org.)

The charts shown in Figure 8-2 come from classic works in building learning taxonomies.

Figure 8-2. Comparison of two taxonomy of skills charts.

Bloom's Taxonomy of Skills in the Cognitive Domain	*Simpson's Taxonomy of Skills in the Psychomotor Domain*
From lowest to highest:	*From lowest to highest:*
Knowledge	Perception
Comprehension	Preparation
Application	Guided response
Analysis	Pattern
Synthesis	Performance
Evaluation	

Source: Based on B. S. Bloom, *Taxonomy of Educational Objectives,* book 1, *Cognitive Domain* (New York: Longmans, 1954). E. J. Simpson, *The Classification of Objectives, Psychomotor Domain* (Urbana, IL: University of Illinois, 1966).

4. Dealing with Various Learning Styles

The following guidelines will help you design your training to accommodate various learning styles you might expect in a classroom full of individual learners. They will also be helpful in designing one-on-one or peer training, where the trainee could be expected to have a preference for one learning style over another. Instructional designers need to remember that each adult has developed, perhaps unconsciously, a style of learning that's unique for that person. This learning style is based on an individual's values, family influences, personality, work experiences, and past learning successes. The guidelines will remind you of the many considerations regarding learning style.

1. Present information that appeals to "left-brained" preferences— that is, sequential, logical, organized information that requires reasoned analysis to understand.

2. Present information that appeals to "right-brained" preferences—that is, nonverbal stimuli, impulsive, simultaneous, messy information requiring intuition and synthesis to understand.

3. Build in opportunities for divergent thinking—generating hypotheses, being creative, and solving problems using the concept of what might be possible.

4. Build in opportunities for convergent thinking—gathering evidence, documenting, and solving problems by figuring out observable necessary components.

5. Teach students to look for patterns—in verbal expression, in visual information, in situations in which touching, hearing, or smelling are important to the job.

6. Teach students to understand analogies and use them to foster understanding of new concepts and skills.

7. Build in opportunities for quiet individual work as well as noisy group work.

8. Encourage team problem solving in small groups so that trainees can learn from each other and can develop experience working with learners of varying style preferences.

9. Train your instructors to learn to listen for clues to a person's preferred style—for example, "I see," "I believe," "I hear," "I figure," "I can prove."

10. Appreciate that in the same class you'll have students on the same issue who'll want to ask you "what" and others who will always want to ask you "why," and that both approaches are equally valid. Be sure that your instructors are prepared to satisfy each kind of question—sometimes coming from the same person.

11. Build in opportunities for individuals to exercise the various kinds of memory involved in human information processing—the short-term memory of present information delivered by current sensory inputs, the information store of past experiences in long-term memory, and the process of associating the present and the past. Be sure that training is consciously designed and delivered to support both short-term and long-term memory.

12. Build in the opportunity for trainees to plan as well as to "shoot from the hip."

5. Design Standards for Various Parts of a Course

The following lists of standards can be useful in several ways: you can use them in checklist fashion as you design training, or you can incorporate them into an evaluation form for trainees or other evaluators to use at the conclusion of class or at the end of training development. The lists can be used by individuals or as discussion documents during design reviews.

Standards for classroom training

1. *Objectives*
   - Appropriate to the job the trainee must do
   - Learnable
   - Pitched at the right level
   - Organized to facilitate learning
   - Clearly stated
   - Measurable
2. *Content*
   - Current
   - Accurate
   - Adequate in scope
   - Sequenced properly
   - Relevant to the trainee's job
3. *Course Setting*
   - Comfortable
   - Safe (ergonomically correct, physically and psychologically secure)
   - Accessible course materials
   - Adequate in equipment and quality of manuals, tools, audiovisual aids
4. *Instructor's Delivery*
   - Sticks to the timing and daily agenda of lessons
   - Demonstrates an engaging presentation style
   - Encourages trainee participation
   - Values trainee contributions
   - Credible content mastery
   - Obviously prepared
5. *Training Materials*
   - Appropriate readability level in trainee manuals (not too many long sentences and five-syllable words)
   - Consistent in format of information in trainee manuals
   - Clean lines, high quality graphics
   - Accurate and consistent labels in figures and tables, on slides and transparencies (often a problem when several designers are working independently on parts

of a course or slides are purchased from vendors who label things differently from the way your company labels them)

- Visually attractive
- Easy to handle and use
- Accurate in emphasis and content of promotional materials

6. *Instructional Media*
   - Videotape and slides: true colors, synchronized audio, instructional purpose in terms of camera work and narrative, images sequenced properly for learning, appropriate image size and clarity, white space around letters and words
   - Transparencies: readability (be careful of handwritten ones), white space and lack of clutter, purposeful (that is, not simply a duplication of what you say; transparencies should reinforce, illustrate, and complement instruction; well-designed instruction should drive the transparencies, not the other way around)

Standards for computer-based training[1]

1. *Human Factors and Human-Machine Interface*
   - Help command always available
   - High rate of relevant trainee response options
   - Consistent formats of prompts, instructions, error messages, command inputs, and so on
   - No scrolling evident
   - Highlighting consistent in its purpose
   - Restart easy and fast
   - Response time appropriately controlled
   - Good readability of text, labels, numbers

2. *Instructional Design*
   - Program accomplishes learner objectives
   - Interactive lessons exercise trainees on the appropriate skill
   - Feedback designed into the correct places
   - Test results continually accessible to trainees
   - Instruction clear
   - Higher-level skills taught whenever possible
   - Linkages made to prior knowledge
   - Learning options plentiful in each lesson

[1] From *Training Workbook & Kit* by Carolyn Nilson, 1989. Reprinted with permission of the publisher, Prentice Hall Direct A Division of ARCO.

3. *Presentation*
   - Branching to encourage problem solving evident
   - Text broken into appropriate steps or segments
   - Enough white space on screens
   - Most of introductory sections of each lesson trainee controlled

6. Lesson Plan Format

The formats of the lesson plans shown in Figures 8-3 and 8-4 suggest the two most common ways to document lessons. Trainers often group together a set of lesson plans and call it the instructor guide. Instructors who are subject matter experts or who are experienced in dealing with the lesson content can easily teach from these kinds of lesson plans. The formats contain the same information; they are simply rotated, one is in vertical format, the other, horizontal format.

Figure 8-3. A lesson plan in vertical format.

Lesson title	Delivery time

Materials and AV equipment needed

Learner objectives

  1. _____

  2. _____

Content outline

  1. _____

     A. _____

     B. _____

  2. _____

     A. _____

     B. _____

     C. _____

  3. _____

Figure 8-4. A lesson plan in horizontal format.

Lesson title   Delivery time

Learner Objectives

1. _____

2. _____

Content Outline   **Materials and AV Equipment Needed**

  1. _____   _____

     A. _____   _____

     B. _____   _____

  2. _____   _____

     A. _____   _____

     B. _____   _____

     C. _____   _____

  3. _____   _____

7. Worksheet for Writing Objectives

Very often in the process of designing training, you begin by establishing *what* should be learned (the content) and then specifying *how* it should be learned (the objectives for the learner). Documentation is based on the following formula (see Figure 8-5) for creating an objective:

Do this_____ To this_____ In this amount

Figure 8-5. Example of formula for creating an objective.

Call up ...   ... the online   ... each time you
                       HELP screen ...   activate a function key.

Note: Training must be designed to address the needs of each part of the objective: procedures for calling up; meaning of items on the HELP screen, contrasts with other screens, analogies to human help, cross-references to help in user manuals and computer documentation; overview of the purpose of function keys; built-in practice time; and a tally sheet to record correct responses and instructions on how to record self-evaluation tallies.

When you engage in design reviews of initial course design efforts, the worksheet shown in Figure 8-6 can be helpful. The review team can use the form to validate the basics of your course design. It's a good idea to review all the objectives of a unit of instruction (group of lessons) side by side with the content outline of that same unit. Figure 8-6 provides space to list all of a unit's objectives, that is, several from each lesson plan that the unit comprises.

Figure 8-6. Worksheet for listing objectives in unit of instruction.

Learner Objectives for Unit

No.   Title

Lesson Title	Do this ...	... to this ...	... in this amount.
1:			
2:			
3:			
4:			
5:			

Typical Application of Training Design in the Growing Business

The course that resulted from the instructional design process described in the following case study has been used in a variety of businesses: a fashion design company, a real estate office, a packaging company, an engineering company, a software development company, and a public relations firm. It has also been used in the business curriculum of a community adult school. The course was created in response to the need of a particular company, then adapted to the needs of other companies.

How One Instructional Designer Went About Designing Literacy Training

This design case study is presented in chart form. It highlights the issues in instructional design and lists the actions chosen to address these issues. Note that some are training issues, and some are not. This case will help you get inside the mind of an instructional designer.

Issues	Deliberations and Actions
1. These are the *business reasons* for wanting this course: • Too much time is spent rewriting, getting approvals, entering data. • There are too many meetings—improved written communication could save time and be used instead of meeting. • There are internal customer complaints about poor quality of memos, documentation, and writing in general—too much secretarial time devoted to correcting errors that should not	1. Timing concerns seem to be a major driver of complaints; any new course will have to be concise and delivered efficiently. 2. There seems to be a lack of standards for in-house communication. Check into this; if none exist, develop them, and perhaps include a few lessons on standards for writing in this course. 3. Find out why nobody pays any attention to the style manual. Scrap it or get somebody to revise it. Suspect lack of practice opportunity, lack of cues to facilitate remembering. Probably recast this as a

Issues	Deliberations and Actions
have been made by persons generating written documents.	course. (It's trying to be a self-help book but has none of the elements of designs for learning in it.)
• People around here are too wordy—we're wasting paper and the time to generate it.	4. Develop a writing skills analysis questionnaire for all target employees so
• Nobody pays any attention to the style manual; therefore, there's no consistency in the way people write.	they can tell us where their problems are. Pay special attention to structure of sentences, tense, agreement, punctuation, use of
2. The *content* should probably be geared to whatever it is that supports effective written communication.	parallel expression, and word choice.
• We need to find out how much employees already know about effective business writing and where the gaps are.	5. Do a sample check of reading skills—poor reading ability often is related to poor writing ability.
	6. Organize the content into grammar skills and composition skills. Figure out which skills are easiest to learn; arrange them hierarchically.
• We need to find out who (what types of employees) are the most "needy" and the areas of deficiency.	7. Use examples from the company to make the course seem real, and not a high school remedial
• We want samples of documents that cause the complaints.	course.
3. Objectives	8. Use the data-collecting activities to make more
• It's easy to get off on the wrong track regarding objectives. Many high-level people don't know the basics of grammar and style, so many objectives will have to be at a low or basic	people aware of the need; get verification from many different sources. Share both the problem and the solution.
	9. Getting the objectives right is the major challenge of this course. They have to

Continued on page 170

Continued from page 169

Issues	Deliberations and Actions

level. We can't be blinded by the fact that high-level people and well-educated employees lack some basic skills.
 	
4. Delivery
   • The choice of delivery method is important because these trainees will be very aware of how much time and money are being consumed on basic skills. They'll tend to have a "shoot the messenger" frame of mind, and will insist on very cost-effective training.
   • Instructor presence is required and individual attention is a must. The choice of instructor will also be critical; it must be someone who is kind, tough regarding content, and gives constant reinforcing feedback.
	be at a low level in terms of cognitive structure (that is, recognizing, recalling, labeling), but they also have to contain a strong dose of analysis and evaluation because many of the potential trainees are people in responsible positions who are used to doing analytical and higher level work every day—they just can't write.
	
	10. This is one of those strange situations in which supportive feedback must occur about every 10 minutes. Trainees will be embarrassed to admit that they can't write, so the course will have to be set up in such a way that they can practice all the time, under supportive instructional supervision while they are unlearning their bad habits and relearning the rules and conventions of business writing.
	
	11. These are some delivery options: peer tutoring in small groups, classroom training with "breakout" rooms for intense small group work with facilitators, one-on-one training, and coaching.

Other Design Issues as the Course Developed

As the course design progressed, there were the issues of what kind of trainee materials to use—what proportion of real documents from the company and what proportion from current business magazines, newspapers, and textbooks. There was the issue of learning style; in a topic such as this, there will probably be very strong opinions and approaches about learning (for example, "I never could write essays"; "I hated to memorize spelling words"; "I loved diagramming sentences—don't they do that anymore?"; or "Why can't we just use e-mail?"). There was also the issue of how many throwaway practice exercises, as compared with permanent job aids, should be taken back to the desk. Finally, there was the issue of possible culture bias in the specification of standards.

Stay with the Program

All the issues discussed in the chart and in the previous section illustrate the design component in ISD, the standard system for creating training in a business of any size. Particularly in the growing business or the merged and recombined business, when the pulls and pressures of expansion are competing with time and resources for everything else, it's critical for the person in charge of training to follow the ISD model—to stay with the program. The quick or cheap solution to skills and knowledge gaps just won't get the job done, and those expansion pulls and pressures will put training out of business.

Good design is the heart of good training. Training as a start-up operation has a wonderful opportunity to grow with the business— to build quality into products and processes, to meet the challenges of a diverse work force, to raise the individual's capacity for creative thinking and problem solving, and to substantially contribute to your company's ability to stay in business. Training is the human resources program of choice for the millennium.

Chapter 9

Delivery Options and Presentation Tips

There are many good books to buy and numerous seminars to attend on how to stand up in front of a group and do a presentation, give a speech, or teach a class. Rather than duplicate these "technique" approaches, this chapter helps you to decide what kind of delivery mode to choose by focusing on the relationship of delivery of training to its design and to your business goals.

This chapter lets you see the possibilities for delivering the best training with your available resources, and any tips for presenting training are suggested within this framework of options. Training delivery is seen as part of a larger training "system," consistent with your company's strategic directions.

Delivery as Part of a Training System

The first thing you should remember is that the delivery of instruction is only one part of the whole experience of training. Before you get to the actual phase of delivering training, you will have spent considerable time in analysis of who needs what and for what specific job purposes, and you will have either designed and written a course yourself, hired someone else to write it for you, or chosen a prepackaged course from a catalog, a salesperson, or in response to a promotional flyer.

After the course is finished, you still have work to do too. The training experience doesn't stop at the end of the teaching; the experience of learning in a structured environment is always followed up by some kind of evaluation of that experience, by some kind of personal contact when the employee gets back on the job, and by feeding back the post-training suggestions of employees into the analysis phase, which starts the cycle over again for the next time. The training itself actually comes in the middle of the full cycle that includes analysis, design, development, and evaluation, as shown in the model in Figure 9-1.

Figure 9-1. Training delivery as a component of the instructional system.

The Instructional System Design (ISD) Model

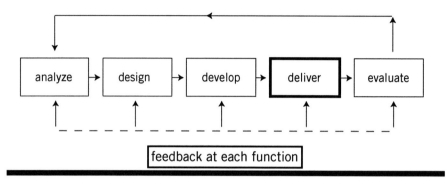

When you place training delivery in the context of a broader training system, you realize that choosing the right mode of presenting training is a very important function of the training manager. The right kind of delivery will depend upon upfront analysis (needs assessment); an accurate and high-quality analysis will point you toward the most appropriate choice of delivery mode.

With the ideal delivery mode made obvious by your needs assessment, your training can be designed with a sense of conservatism, with no unnecessary information or frivolous processes written into it. With the hard reality of dollar constraints in mind, and business goals foremost, the design and delivery choices can mesh together to provide interesting, on-target, cost-effective training. Think "need to know" rather than "nice to know."

Never throw a seminar, classroom, videotape, or online learning experience at an audience because you think the topic is something everybody really has to know or because the instructor has a great reputation or the salesperson was especially convincing and bought you a terrific lunch.

It's a great temptation to fall back on the old models of sending folks away for three days, of getting a classroom full of students together, or of shipping around a videotape. These all might be fine, but they also might all be a colossal waste of time and an unwarranted drain on your budget. The point is that you want training to be as spare as possible, directed at a very specific need of very individual employees. Taking the time to thoughtfully assess your delivery options, based on good needs analysis and design information, will allow you to use the presentation of train-

ing to accomplish your business goals. The wrong training presented in the wrong way will haunt you—and cost you—forever.

These are some of the things you'll have to consider when
choosing the right delivery mode:

- *Objectives for the Training.* Does this delivery mode support
  these objectives? Can we actually accomplish these objectives by doing the course this way?
- *Daily Agenda of the Training.* What should blocks of instruction look like? Should there be a change every two hours?
  Will trainees get bored with the delivery plan?
- *Lapse Time for the Training.* Is there enough instructional
  time built into this training? Is the total time allotted for
  the course enough to accomplish our objectives? Is "time
  on task" sufficient for learning in depth? Is time wasted by
  the format of the delivery? Does the medium get in the
  way of the message?
- *Quality of the Instructor.* Is the best instructor available to
  deliver this particular training? In self-study, is the instructional design (the implied instructor) strong and effective
  for this kind of delivery option?
- *Transfer of Skills Back to the Job.* Does this choice of delivery
  facilitate the trainee's ability to use newly learned skills
  after training is over? Is there enough reality built into the
  delivery of training so that employees see the need to
  "transfer" from the learning situation to the work situation?
- *Employee Preference.* Have you considered what the potential
  trainees themselves prefer? Do their work schedules suggest
  one mode of delivery over another? Have you considered
  their commitments? Have you asked them how they learn
  best? Are you truly learner-centered in your choice of delivery, or can you be accused of delivering training according
  to your own "administrative" convenience?

Surveying the Possibilities

The following section presents three basic categories of delivery
options and details the choices within each. You see a description
of the option, the reason why you might choose one over another,
and the resources you'll need to commit if you choose this option.
These "big three" training delivery groups are supervised on-the-job
training, independent or self-study, and group training.

Supervised On-the-Job Training

This mode of delivering training is probably the one that is chosen, consciously or unconsciously, by most people who need to train someone at work. Supervisors, for example, often perform the function of instructor for new employees who report to them, employees coming back from sick leave, employees rotating into a department, and employees who need to upgrade their skills or their knowledge—about a critical business procedure, new product, organizational change, or customer. Managers often assign others to function as instructors on the job.

Supervised on-the-job training must be planned with as much care as a course delivered to a group in a classroom. If you want the training to be aimed at the right target, spare yet sufficient in design, and delivered in such a way that learning happens and you don't waste time, it must be carefully planned. Remember that supervised on-the-job training requires the time of three people: you or another supervisor, the employee who's the trainee, and the employee who's the trainer.

If this kind of training doesn't go well, you end up with two potentially high performers who are frustrated, an aborted working relationship that you'd hoped would lead to increased productivity, and your own time invested in a bad deal. Poorly delivered on-the-job training can end up taking huge amounts of time away from the job itself, and it can result in great confusion about when training ends and the job begins. The stakes can be high in supervised on-the-job training, so you want to be sure that it is designed and delivered well.

One-on-one training

One-on-one training is training delivered to an individual employee by another individual, often by someone in a management relationship to the trainee.

You choose this delivery option when the trainee can benefit the most from the personal interaction with the specific trainer, when the trainer is truly excellent as a teacher and as a worker, when the thing that must be taught and learned is clearly related to the skills of the trainee's job, and when business reasons dictate that the trainee is needed more on the job than in a classroom interacting with other employees.

Resources you'll need to commit to a one-on-one delivery are generally minimal, but do include some preparation time on the part of the instructor. You'll want to be sure that the person who's going to become a trainer works from a content outline and learning objectives for each training session. You'll want to be sure that your trainer provides "course" materials or a notebook for the trainee and that these are of good quality. If the trainer is not you yourself, you might want to plan some time to sit down with the trainer to review the training documents for clarity, inclusiveness, accuracy, and approach. You might need to find a quiet place for training to occur, if it can't be done at the trainee's or the trainer's job site. You'll want to be sure that instructional media and supplies, such as a VCR or flipchart, are available for use during training and that your instructor is supported with clerical help during preparation and phone coverage while actually doing the training.

Peer training

Peer training is instruction delivered to an employee or group of employees by their fellow employees. Peer training can be one-on-one or group-based training. Its key characteristic is that employees have chosen to become trainers for a short time to deliver training to their co-workers.

You choose this delivery option when you believe that the special relationship of "we're in this together" can be instrumental in accomplishing the objectives for the training, when you have corporate values or specialized procedures that are best transmitted at the peer level and not "from above," and when you have employees who are competent and interested in being peer trainers. Peer training can have good spinoffs in improved communications, shared values, and esprit de corps.

Resource commitments are similar to those detailed above in the section on one-on-one training. In addition, if you choose to develop a peer training program with groups of people, you'll need more classroom space, course materials, and media equipment. Classroom training also requires more time away from the job, so if you are a job shop that assigns time to "overhead" instead of to client project numbers or operational codes, you'll need to be prepared to commit these time allocations for both the trainers and the trainees while they're in class. A peer training program will also probably require some train-the-trainer instruction for the employees you've chosen to be peer trainers, either by yourself, by a consultant who comes to you, or through an off-site seminar. You'll also need to provide some kind of evaluation and feedback to the peer trainers, so figure on time to develop standards of instruction, a monitoring plan, and a feedback process.

Mentoring and coaching

Mentoring and coaching are forms of supervised on-the-job training that focus on an employee's development. Although coaching is often seen as the shorter-term approach, and often based on a specific challenge or problem, mentoring is generally seen as a longer-term approach to helping an employee become the best possible worker. Mentoring and coaching are training based on a combination of the "expert" model and a counseling approach. In these highly personalized training approaches, a deliberate and often extended relationship between coach or mentor and trainee is set up and monitored.

You choose mentoring when you have a more senior or more experienced and highly competent employee in the same field as a newer employee or an employee whom you think would benefit from the kind of training a mentor can provide. In your choice of mentor, you'll want to be sure that the person enjoys sharing information and giving support to a less experienced person; not everyone does. You'll want to be sure that your mentor is not just a big talker and that he or she can assume the roles that an instructor must assume. You'll want to be sure that your mentor is a patient person who can keep confidences when appropriate. You'll want to be sure that your mentor truly has the company's well-being in mind and will not be threatened by possibly having his or her trainee excel and outperform the mentor. You'll want someone who is well-organized and can stick to a development plan on behalf of someone else. Your mentor must be a good listener, a good analyst, and a perceptive distinguisher between fact and opinion.

A mentor's job should have a beginning and an end, so you'll want someone in the position who can handle the psychological separation from a learning situation that is often characterized by intensity, extended and deepening trust, and generous give and take. If you're not ready to deal with the psychological spinoffs of mentoring, or believe that your employees won't be able to separate the instructional intent from the friendship aspects of mentoring, don't get involved in the first place. If you like the idea of the highly personalized approach, go for the shorter-term coaching instead, and base your trainer-trainee relationship on a specific and timely problem that can be most effectively solved by this combination of expert advice and counseling.

Resource commitments are basically the resources of time, spread out over the mentoring period (three months, six months, one year). Mentors often spend considerable time with their trainees especially if their personalities are well-matched. You'll probably want to suggest some mentoring time guidelines, such as about 15 percent of one's time to be spent in mentoring duties. By setting some guidelines, you'll be able to monitor both the time and effectiveness of mentoring encounters, and you'll be able to assign a dollar figure to the mentoring training based on the mentor's and the trainee's salaries.

Cross-training

Cross-training is supervised on-the-job training that capitalizes on the proven idea that adults learn well from experience and from each other. It is training that places the trainee in the job situation of another worker, usually in a different but related job, for a temporary period of time for the express purpose of learning the essentials of that different job. Good cross-training has objectives for the learner, a plan for instruction, an evaluation and feedback process, and someone in charge of the learning. It is not job rotation, nor is it filling in for someone on leave. It's training, with all of the "instructional system" relationships of training delivery.

You choose this delivery option when you believe that the immersion approach is the one that will pay off in more effective learning. Cross-training is usually multiskill in focus and is a good choice when you want the trainee to observe and try out in a hands-on, reality-based fashion just exactly how the job is done.

The resource you'll need to commit is the time away from the job. You might want to plan a cross-training program for several employees at once, each spending time in another job, so that all jobs are "covered," even if it means being covered by a trainee. Because cross-training is generally within related jobs, you'll still get some productive time from each trainee in cross-training, making it a cost-effective approach to on-the-job training. The cross-training experience is often facilitated by the use of a checklist to be used by the trainee as he or she assumes the role of another job. You'll have to allow the time and staff expertise to construct such a checklist of key concepts about the job, procedures to be followed, skill requirements, reporting relationships, typical pitfalls and performance problem areas, etc. The combination of being immersed in the job, allowing the trainee to be in charge of the challenge, trusting the employee to perform to the best of his or her ability in a new situation, plus having a visual checklist to follow, often is the formula for very successful training.

Independent Study

An increasingly popular mode of delivering training during these times of change and uncertainty about the numbers (or lack of numbers) of employees is independent study, often called self-study. If your company does not have the opportunity for economies of scale by offering classrooms full of training, if training delivery staff is at a minimum, if supervisors are already doing double duty, and you choose not to embark on any kind of employee-to-employee training, you might want to consider developing an independent study training program. The most common types of independent study delivery are videotape and interactive video, computer-based training, and taking courses on the Internet.

There are several obvious advantages to independent study: Trainees can study in their own best time slots and in private; you don't need an instructor; often the training materials can be rotated and shared among the trainees (as in a videotape that circulates from a tape library).

And, of course, there are some disadvantages. Packaged programs tend to be aimed at an average trainee. An individualized needs assessment for your particular company seldom has preceded the design and development of the training program or video, so there's a pretty good chance that the self-study program will have extraneous and irrelevant information in it. This means that your trainees will have to be smart enough and patient enough to fast-forward through the parts of the training that they don't need—in short, they'll have to know what they don't need to know, and that's unlikely. It's easy for trainees who are above the average to feel frustrated or bored with self-study, and for those below the average to get lost and give up. In self-study, the burden is on you as the training provider to carefully choose the kind of self-study program that does in fact meet your employees' needs. Self-study can be a time waster and a poor investment if it doesn't match the level of your trainees and their specific problems that you want training to address. Cost-effective training delivery requires a good match.

Self-study programs are not right for many employees. Many workers today have grown up in a media-rich environment that has provided entertainment and information. Most employees associate video and electronic media with these functions, not with learning. It is a mistake to equate information with education and learning. Learning requires a very different design and delivery from the design and delivery of information or entertainment. It's easy for today's employee—and sometimes today's training managers—to give lip service to training when what really is happening is entertainment or information dissemination. With electronic self-study delivery systems, you have to be especially careful that the packages you buy lead your employees to learning, not simply to interesting or entertaining diversions. Employees are used to being entertained by videos and by computer games, so be careful that your chosen electronic self-study medium does not unwittingly carry with it the passivity that generally accompanies TV or video entertainment.

The wary training manager will also realize that the production of training videos and computer-based training courses varies greatly from source to source. If a well-trained and experienced instructional designer, instructor, and evaluator have been involved in creating the course, your chances of obtaining an instructional program are enhanced. If you are not sure about this, your best defense is to have the program previewed and evaluated by an instructional designer before you purchase it, even if it means hiring an instructional design consultant for a few hours to help you do the assessment. It's very easy to get "taken in" by slick promotion and fancy features. If you want an instructional program that leads to learning, then be sure that your self-study course is, in fact, a course—a learning opportunity, not an information dump or entertainment.

Another option in self-study is the old-fashioned correspondence course—the kind that is based on a series of workbooks and mailed corrective comments from an instructor who works out of an office in a correspondence school. Today's correspondence courses come with a variety of enhancements, such as videotapes or audiotapes, simulations, models, computer diskettes, and fax numbers. Companies often create their own workbook-based courses disseminated through the corporate mail system.

As in the electronic versions, this kind of independent study requires a self-motivated trainee and good instructional design. Its major advantage is that it is print-based, book-based, and comes "wrapped" in the expectancies that most employees have about learning. As with the electronic options, the instructor's role is distant or invisible on a day-to-day, minute-to-minute basis. There's no one to tell the trainee that he or she is doing a great job or perhaps ought to try the solution in another way. There's no one to give support through eye contact. There's no instructor to smile at trainees during the tough times. There's no one to test a trainee on the spot and suggest that maybe he or she knows enough about this topic and can securely go forward with the next concept or skill. There's no instructor to suggest networking with another trainee several seats away or with a former trainee in the next building.

Both ASTD and *Training* magazine's 1998 end of year surveys of the industry show an increase over the last few years in the percentage of training delivered by computer, and, more importantly, a huge percentage increase over the immediate past year. ASTD in its "1999 State of the Industry Report" (*Training & Development*, January 1999), for example, reported that the typical firm in 1996 delivered only 6 percent of its training using learning technologies, but in 1997 delivered 9 percent. Companies defined as "leading edge" companies in 1997 delivered nearly 12 percent of its training using learning technologies. By the year 2000, the average firm expects around 22 percent of its training to be delivered using learning technologies; 27 percent for leading-edge companies. *Training* magazine puts the average number at 19 percent.

This trend indicates that self-study is likely to be the learning structure through which employees learn online; and if this trend continues, at the turn of the century, conservatively speaking, about one-fifth to one-quarter of training will be this kind of computer-mediated self-study.

ASTD's 1997 *Training Benchmarking Report* makes a useful distinction between presentation methods and distribution methods. Training managers need to be clear in their own heads about the differences. Use this chart to clarify your thinking:

Presentation Methods

- ☐ CBT, text only
- ☐ Multimedia
- ☐ Interactive TV
- ☐ Teleconferencing
- ☐ Groupware

- ☐ Virtual Reality
- ☐ Electronic Performance Support Systems (EPSS)

Distribution Methods

- ☐ Cable TV
- ☐ CD-ROM
- ☐ Electronic Mail (e-mail)
- ☐ Extranet
- ☐ Internet
- ☐ Intranet
- ☐ Local Area Network
- ☐ Satellite TV
- ☐ Simulator
- ☐ Voice Mail
- ☐ Wide Area Network
- ☐ World Wide Web

Although good CBT, interactive video training, and Web-based training will build in some branching and feedback, for most trainees this is not enough. Most employees prefer a person to be available during learning; with most people, it seems to happen best in concert with at least one other person. Learning can be lonely, risky, and somewhat frightening. If you choose independent self-study, be sure that you weigh the time advantages against the necessity for in-depth pre-evaluation to ensure appropriate and adequate *instructional* design and delivery. Know the differences between information, entertainment, play, and learning designs.

Group Training

Classroom training, either in a workplace training room or a rented hotel auditorium or conference center, is the kind of training that most employees think of when they think about training. This is the most efficient kind of training when it's done well, because one instructor can serve many trainees at once, and the dynamics of the group can facilitate the learning and transfer of newly learned skills and knowledge back to the jobs of class attendees.

If classroom training is done poorly, it is a huge waste of money, especially if you've sent your employees off to an out-of-town seminar and travel and living costs are incurred as part of the training expense too.

Classroom training is the model for delivery of instruction with which most employees are familiar. In the traditional model of classroom training, the instruction is teacher-led and subject-centered (driven by the sequential arrangement of topics within the subject). In the workplace adaptation of this traditional model of group training, the focus shifts to the learner and the specific information or skill needs of that learner. In a group of adults at work, obviously, there will be many variations of needs around the same subject, therefore shifting the traditional role of the teacher-leader to that of the teacher-facilitator. Training is *teacher-facilitated* and *learner-centered.*

When you make the decision to run a class, be sure that your instructor can deliver training in this facilitative mode. A good trainer will pay at least as much attention to the "process" aspects of the course as the "content" aspects. If possible, before you engage an instructor for classroom training, observe that person in action to be sure that he or she is in fact able to handle the diversity of individuals in the group and that he or she doesn't fall back on the old model of pedagogical teacher-led instruction. The old model simply doesn't work for adults who need to learn something.

When you consider group training, think in broad terms that include accomplishing training objectives through other group endeavors such as off-site hands-on workshops, field trips, and conferences. The clue here in considering these other kinds of group activities as possible training delivery modes is to look at the learning needs of your employees, establish learning objectives for them, and take it from there. If group training is the best option for accomplishing those learning objectives, then perhaps one of these alternative group delivery modes is a good choice for you. The thing that makes training, and not just a day away from the office, is the merge of the training need with reasonable and doable objectives. Don't overlook workshops, field trips, seminar groups online, and conferences as possibilities for effective group training. Group-based training also can be conducted using e-mail, chat groups, listservs, and instructor-moderated online lessons. Check your local college for online learning models.

Remember—These Students Are Grown-Ups

Never lose sight of the fact that trainees at work are adults. They've done many responsible and successful things during their lifetimes, including getting and performing their jobs. Their employers (and your employer), their families, their friends, and society at large have all told them in various ways that they are valued contributors to the forward movement of life. These trainees are grown-ups and must be treated as such.

Adult learners have certain specialized needs as learners. They want to know exactly why they need to learn something, so be sure to relate the training to a specific job-related challenge or problem. Adults won't take the time for training that they perceive as irrelevant to their work. They basically come to work to work, not to go to school. Adult students like to tell others what they know and to exhibit competence; they prefer to be active, not passive, during training. Adult egos become very fragile in a learning situation; often they must admit that they don't know something or that they have been doing something poorly. Good training delivery will compensate for the ego loss by validating the trainee's competence. Adult learners like surety, knowing that they're doing it right, and accomplishing what's expected of them. Good delivery will include checklists, written procedures, "how to" instructions, and perhaps a job aid or chart to take back to the job as a reminder.

Customer Training

A sometimes-overlooked training essential is the delivery of training to customers. Computer software–intensive start-up companies with that special software niche or online service are absolutely dependent upon customers knowing how to use their products. Often this means new companies are faced with the dual training delivery problem of internal training of one's staff and customer service staff, as well as training of one's customers and even potential customers. Good customer training has big payoffs in terms of getting and holding onto customers.

One company that is doing customer training right is PATRIOT PROPERTIES, INC. of Peabody, Massachusetts. The company's most visible product is its *AssessPro 4.0* professional appraisal software, a Windows-based system for towns, cities, and counties to assess their real estate and personal property for the purpose of tax assessment in compliance with state laws. Patriot Properties has been in business since 1985, initially with a DOS-based system, now listing customers in nine different states.

Like many service companies of the 1990s, Patriot Properties' success as a business enterprise depends not only on the quality of its product but also on the ability of its customers to fully use the company's software and the company's resident expertise—and so it depends on the quality of the training that Patriot Properties delivers to those customers. Patriot Properties' customers number around 120, primarily municipalities in Massachusetts.

Like many other small, technology-intensive companies, Patriot Properties (40 employees) also offers other related services, such as consulting services to help towns maintain current market values and prepare for state-mandated revaluation of properties and for annual reviews; and "field work" personnel to provide residential, industrial, and commercial property review and individual unimproved parcel review. Key to the ability of assessors being able to do their jobs of assessing, however, is local ability to use Patriot Properties' *AssessPro 4.0* software.

The informational brochure describing the software indicates that it has these features: ease of use, compatibility, multiple valuation options, sketching, video imaging, public access screen, Geographical Information Systems capability, and report writing. It also notes that the system's "Quicklist" and "Filter" innovations offer efficiencies unavailable in text-based systems, and that the "fully networkable" system has the power and flexibility to service a municipality of virtually any size. These words alone present some rather hefty training delivery challenges.

Patriot Properties' customers vary widely in their computer literacy. Some small town assessors are unpaid, many are retired from "other" jobs and paid a token salary; some are compensated adequately; some do paid consulting on the side. In short, the person of "the assessor" varies widely. Some have offices and staff; others do not. The nature of the parcel count also varies widely from municipality to municipality. Patriot Properties' customers in Massachusetts include New Bedford, with 28,000 parcels; Haverhill, with 20,000 parcels; and Rowe and Mt. Washington, with only about 500 parcels each. Outside of Massachusetts, customers also vary widely: Sarasota County, Florida, with 273,000 parcels; Nashville, Tennessee, with 235,000 parcels; Lucas County, Ohio, with 160,000 parcels; Washoe County, Nevada, with 120,000 parcels; and Racine, Wisconsin, with 27,000 parcels. It is to Patriot Properties' advantage to make its software work for everyone; that is, to enable and facilitate these widely disparate customers to use *AssessPro 4.0.* Patriot Properties' Web site boasts, "We have converted over 40 clients from our three leading regional competitors, and they have converted none of our clients"; and "...converted data from 11 different assessing systems and interfaced with 21 different tax collection systems." This is a company that is customer-focused and growth-oriented.

Another brochure explains that the company has made the software as user-friendly as possible by using large icons, smart icons, interactive help, context-sensitive brief help, and a complete online user manual for ready reference. Demonstrations are available online and proceed at the customer's pace (www.patriotproperties.com). The Web site's "Company History" description spells out its approach: "The data processing staff works closely with the project supervisor and client to customize software products for each installation. Data processing conforms to the project's requirements, not the converse. These two differences make for a sensitive and responsive environment for the client."

Patriot Properties encourages individual self-study and experimentation with the system; they also maintain an active and accessible Help Desk. A toll-free 800 number is fully staffed between 8 a.m. and 5 p.m. daily. An interview with a customer, Noel Nilson, chairman of the Board of Assessors of the town of Sandisfield, Massachusetts (1,600 parcels), presents customer training from the receiver's point of view. Nilson says, "They solve problems. If you are desperate, they are desperate. This customer orientation is crucial to their success. Their people have been trained to keep their cool; they've also been trained to learn from the customer in order to give even more effective service the next time around." Patriot Properties also provides five days of one-on-one customer training at the customer's site, an investment of training delivery time and effort well worth it, according to Richard C. Swadel, executive administrator. In development of the software product as well as in its transfer to a specific municipal use, Patriot Properties paid attention to the uniqueness of its individual customers and delivered win-win training that fostered the growth of both the company and the customer. Theirs is a model of customer-centered learning that keeps the company ahead of its competition.

Training the Trainer

Those in charge of training in the growing business often find themselves in the position of having to train their own employees to be trainers. This happens as business grows from no staff in certain departments to full staff. Often, the training manager has to quickly make instructors out of engineers, salespersons, programmers, secretaries, and supervisors of all sorts.

In this situation, many prefer to find a train-the-trainer seminar already developed by a consulting company or college continuing education program and send their would-be trainers to it. Whether you design and teach your own train-the-trainer course or find one already made, here are the topics that should be included:

1. Preparation responsibilities
   - Paperwork such as advertising, registration, writing the catalog entry
   - Placing an order for the right size binders, photocopying handouts, communicating with the printer regarding format, and numbers of course manuals
   - Choosing and ordering refreshments for trainees
   - Scheduling design reviews of course units or modules if the course is a new one or an extensively revised one
   - Placing the course in the master schedule
   - Developing a daily course agenda
2. Options in presenting the course to trainees
   - Web-based training
   - One-on-one instruction
   - EPSS
   - Groups and how they work
   - Labs and experiments
   - How to teach using case studies
   - Role plays and simulations
   - Demonstrations
   - Lectures
   - Distance learning via satellite
3. Physical setup of the classroom
   - Environmental comfort: lights, heat, air
   - Quality of tables and chairs
   - Organization of tables and chairs
   - Electrical hookups: enough of them, conveniently placed, safety (no tripping over cords)
   - Sight lines for projected information

4. Hospitality and creature comforts during training
   - Location of rest rooms
   - Location of lounges and smoking areas
   - Location of telephones
   - Location of message center
   - Location of copying machines
   - Personal computers
   - Location of food and drink
   - Location of emergency and medical help
5. Writing and using lesson plans
   - Format
   - Timing
   - Objectives
   - Specifying media needed for each lesson
6. Choosing and using instructional media
   - Graphic and type style guidelines
   - Use of line, color, motion, sound
   - Nonconfusion of medium and message, that is, media support the content, not supplant it
7. Teaching techniques
   - Questions and answers
   - Active listening
   - Giving feedback
   - Managing conflict
   - Yielding control to trainees; getting it back again
   - Building on trainees' experience
   - Using examples
   - Teaching to objectives
   - Using guided practice, tests, and formative evaluation
   - Using manuals and aids effectively
8. Personal presentation strategies
   - Movement
   - Eye contact
   - Proximity
   - What to do with your hands
   - What to do with your feet
   - Voice
9. How adults learn
   - Motivation
   - Learning styles
   - Responsibility

Tools for Evaluating Training Delivery Systems

The five tools in this section (summarized in Box 9-1) will help you evaluate the key modes of training delivery and help your instructors plan effective instruction. One of the most important management functions you can provide is that of choosing or guiding the choice of the most appropriate delivery medium for the subject to be taught. As a manager, your good judgment regarding the delivery of training can have big payoffs in terms of trainee (customer) satisfaction and resources saved. Each of the five delivery evaluation tools focuses in detail on a major type of training delivery mode. Before matching delivery mode to content to be learned and objectives for the learner, approach the decision of how to deliver training with an open mind. Before accepting on-the-job training, classroom training, a conference, or a computer-based training course, use these tools to sharpen your understanding of how each should work for maximum effectiveness.

Box 9-1. Training delivery tools.

1. *Delivery Tips for On-the-Job Trainers*—Presentation considerations for delivery of four typical on-the-job training challenges: one-on-one, peer, mentoring and coaching, and cross-training

2. *Delivery Dimensions of CBT, IVD, and CD-ROM*—A quality checklist for you to use as you evaluate these electronic delivery modes prior to considering purchase

3. *Principles of Classroom Management*—What to look for in well-delivered group training

4. *Conference Planning PERT Chart*—A chart highlighting the essential planning elements for a successful training conference

5. *Training Follow-up Guidelines*—An outline for facilitating the transfer of skills learned during training to the actual job

---

1. Delivery Tips for On-the-Job Trainers

The chart shown in Figure 9-2 highlights the most critical areas of concern to most on-the-job trainers. This chart will help you anticipate the questions of on-the-job trainers.

Figure 9-2. Presentation considerations for on-the-job training.

Delivery Option	Objectives	Preparation	Content	Evaluation and Feedback
One-on-One	• Keep them simple and few. Try to accomplish only one or two objectives during each lesson. • Stay loose. Be able to incorporate unarticulated objectives that arise during training.	• Find out what "bugs" this specific trainee. Sit down with him or her at least 10 days before planning your training. • Plan the sessions to last one to two hours at most. • Be prepared to give yourself "space" during training; one-on-one gets intense. Design this into the way you deliver the training.	• Be sure you know the parameters of what you're supposed to teach. • Divide up the content into topics. Be sure topics are sequential.	• Encourage the trainee to "try it." Tell him or her, "Yes, that's right" or "No, that's wrong" often during training, and tell the trainee why. • Evaluate and give feedback about every 10 minutes during training. • Don't talk too much. Listen. Let the trainee "talk it out"—give the kind of feedback that helps keep the trainee on target.
Peer	• Keep them simple and few. • Write them down and provide for manager, trainer, trainee joint review. • Tie objectives to 15-minute lessons. Think small; build learning upon learning.	• Be sure the peer trainer's own job is covered while training is going on. • Be sure everyone involved knows when training starts and stops.	• Keep content grounded on shared company values and goals. • Approach training from the view that "we're in this together." • Focus on the ideal outcomes of work processes; show and tell the trainee how to achieve these outcomes.	• Show, tell, demonstrate, and follow procedures. Make checklists and outlines so that both peers (trainer and trainee) can check off items that are finished. • Develop a job competency list of tasks to ensure that peer training will remain focused on work improvement.

Continued on page 192

Continued from page 192

Delivery Option	Objectives	Preparation	Content	Evaluation and Feedback
Mentoring and Coaching	• Think in terms of long-range objectives for the *training* assignment as well as the short-range objectives of each lesson, concept, or specific time together. • Write them down; review them with the person who set up the mentoring, the mentor, and the trainee.	• Interview the trainee's boss regarding the mentoring assignment and how it might affect him or her. Get the trainee's boss on your side before you begin. • As a mentor, decide who the one person is to whom *you* will be responsible for delivering good training.	• Think clearly about the breakdown of skills that you are helping to develop: knowledge, psychomotor skills, or attitude changes.	• Assign general percentages to these types of skills over the course of your mentoring assignment. • Evaluate yourself on how well you're "sticking to the program" (recognize when you are doing other social or task-oriented things). • Develop mentoring success criteria with your trainee. Meet periodically to review progress.
Cross-Training	• Think of objectives for the learner that are related to organization development challenges. • Then develop the specific learning objectives related to the parts of the job. (Use a job description for the ideas.)	• Get all the approvals you need—from supervisors, trainees, and persons whose jobs will be affected by your cross-training efforts. • Know where the similarities and differences are. People learn by relating what's new to what they already know.	• Together with the cross-training location supervisor, develop a content outline and a time frame for the training. Focus on the skills, tasks, and procedures of the job.	• Use a task or skills checklist as an evaluation device. Assign one person the job of observing the trainee and completing the checklist. • Give the trainee a chance for self-evaluation and written comment.

2. Delivery Dimensions of CBT, IVD, and CD-ROM

Use these guidelines for help in choosing computer-based training, interactive videodisc training, and training delivered via CD-ROM.

1. Beware of "bells and whistles" for the sake of bells and whistles. Remind yourself again and again that you're looking for quality instruction, not a display of computer graphics.
2. Be sure that you have enough trainees to make the investment worth it (about 500 trainees over three years).
3. Be sure the vendor is reputable and can provide updates and helpline support over the useful life of the course. One benchmark is a vendor's professional staff turnover—does the vendor in fact pay its high-level development staff enough to keep them over the long haul—and the vendor's ability to give you the service you need over the long haul.
4. Be sure that the topic and photography are current and won't become dated and that the language is nonsexist, free of jargon, and grammatically correct, etc.
5. Be sure that you buy a system that can be easily updated by adding new product information, new procedures, talking heads of new leaders, etc., if you intend to use it for a few years.
6. Be sure that you are aware of all the hardware and software expenses you'll incur. Be sure it's worth it.
7. When you evaluate the instructional design of CBT, IVD, or CD-ROM, ask yourself these essential questions:
    - Is the content right for the medium; that is, can you learn this subject best by this approach?
    - Are the objectives for the learner clear, is instruction obvious toward those objectives, are the objectives attainable through this kind of delivery?
    - Is the system easy to use? Are there menus, help screens, paging, branching, error diagnosis, feedback? Are hardcopy printouts available? Are instructions clear, accurate, and sequential? Is restart sufficient and easy?
    - Are exercises, tests, and feedback nontrivial? Can trainees learn something important from their mistakes?
    - Are test results private and secure in the system?
    - Is the instruction interesting but not "flashy"?
    - Are commands, prompts, and instructions consistent and supportive; that is, do they not get in the way of learning?
    - Are exercises appropriate for the skills to be learned?

- Is feedback at the right places?
- Are high-level skills (application, synthesis, analysis, making judgments) taught as well as low-level skills (identifying, defining, retrieving)?
- Is new information linked conceptually to former information?
- Is the trainee in control of where to start and stop?

3. Principles of Classroom Management

This first set of principles of good delivery focuses on the behavior of the classroom trainer. When you observe instructors managing a group, look for these elements of good instructor performance:

- *Preparation.* The instructor is obviously "on top of things." The instructor knows the objectives, is well-versed in content at mastery level, has handouts and media organized.
- *Planned Start.* The instructor has a structure for the first 15 minutes of class. This includes opening remarks to establish credibility in a nonthreatening way, interactions that help trainees feel comfortable, "advance organizers" that help set the mental stage for the main points of the course, and exercises that yield critical information about what each trainee expects to get out of the course.
- *Lessons.* The instructor presents information in short segments—about 15 minutes each. During this time, the instructor describes, explains, uses examples and analogies, tells what "it isn't" as well as what it is, uses diagrams and demonstrations, asks and answers questions.
- *Formative Evaluation.* As each trainee learns new concepts or skills, during each lesson, the instructor tells that trainee how he or she is doing. Good instruction is always done against a standard. Good instructors are always aware of the standard as well as the individual's proximity to it. (This is why we keep class size small and write in branching and feedback to CBT lessons.)
- *Continuous Feedback.* The instructor seeks feedback from trainees and immediately uses it, being especially adept at modifying a lesson to include up-to-the-minute information of relevance to a trainee's work and individual concerns. The instructor interacts continuously with individual trainees visually and verbally.

This second set of principles of good delivery is a list of classroom management tips for the instructor who is dealing with a group of trainees:

1. Think of a class of trainees as a collection of individuals who will exhibit more differences than likenesses.
2. Give as much attention to managing the group dynamics as you do to delivering the content of the course.
3. Be organized. Practice using instructional materials and media.
4. Learn every student's first name and use it many times during training.
5. Move around; get trainees involved with you and with each other.
6. Use question-and-answer techniques deliberately, alternating between "closed" questions and "open" questions.
7. Listen to your trainees.
8. Give feedback to the class as a whole as well as to individual trainees.
9. If you use handouts and manuals, show the trainees how to use them effectively. Don't just dump them on the class.
10. Prevent problems from arising by using different techniques for facilitating group tasks and group processes.
11. When conflict occurs, manage it.
12. Allow 20 minutes per lesson, but plan on only 15 minutes of instruction. Balance each lesson with explanation, experimentation, and feedback on the trainee's progress.

4. Conference Planning PERT Chart

A conference can be an excellent way of delivering training, as long as your objectives for learning are clear. Before beginning any planning, be sure that all concerned agree that the conference format is the best delivery mode to meet the training needs of your students. Get into the mind-set of thinking of conference attendees as learners.

The PERT chart shown in Figure 9-3 contains simplified conference planning information for the beginning stages of a typical training conference. It is included here as an example of how to use the PERT process to successfully plan a conference. Note that the PERT planning tool shows you what has to be done before going on to other tasks. It indicates relationships and, because of this, is often more useful as a planning tool than a timeline.

Figure 9-3. Use of the PERT process to plan a training conference.

Conference Planning PERT Chart

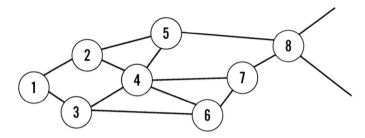

(1)   Do the conference needs assessment, with input from various people (for example, line managers, customers, suppliers); identify the audience; specify learning objectives; choose a title for the conference; choose major topics.

(2)   Choose conference location and set the dates.

(3)   Establish overall budget.

(4)   Name your four-person conference committee—general chairperson and three assistant chairpeople: for management and operations; for speakers and program content; for food and facilities.

(5)   Organize content and prepare preliminary agenda.

(6)   Finalize mailing list for attendees.

(7)   Meet with conference center food staff to set menus and refreshments for breaks.

(8)   Contact potential speakers and group leaders.

5. Training Follow-Up Guidelines

These guidelines will help you turn the training you've just done into productive work:

1. Seek the opinion of your instructor regarding what the trainees actually learned; don't assume that all the course objectives were met. Ask the instructor, not only the students. Also ask your instructors what they hear as they interact with various trainees. Trainers will often pick up cues to organization development issues as well as skill deficiency issues. Use instructors as information channels regarding follow-up.

2. Have the course description and objectives with you when you interview people in follow-up discussions.

3. Include the following questions in any written or online questionnaire or telephone survey:

   - How soon did you use your new knowledge or skill?
   - What elements of training have been most useful on the job?
   - What elements were least useful?
   - What constraints (money, time, support, equipment, systems, schedules, procedures, etc.) have you encountered that prevent you from using what you learned during training?
   - How would you modify the training to make it more useful?
   - What organizational changes would help the application of this training (coaching, peer training, job rotation, mentors, monitoring, reports, supervisor training, support staff, rewards, materials, equipment, spaces, etc.)?

4. In your dialogue with trainees who are now back on the job after training, focus on the higher levels of skills and their importance to the trainee's job. Try to get the trainee to identify the really important skills.

5. Turn evaluation into numbers, that is, frequencies, percentages, dollars, hours, days. "What gets measured gets done" is often true. Employees generally accept the challenge of trying to beat their own best scores.

6. Assign someone the task of being "training monitor."

7. Provide this monitor with forms on which to record comments and observations, and chart progress toward performance standards. Provide the monitor with skills lists.

8. Make it clear that *training* (not the person) is being monitored and evaluated; focus on procedures, timing, and quality of results. Focus on improving training.

9. Highlight and publicize what works.

10. Prepare job aids or dissemination flyers so that others can adapt the successful procedures and techniques to their situations.
11. Keep running lists of trainees' suggestions for making this training better.
12. Use a follow-up form at some regular periodic interval after training. Ask the questions the same way and record responses consistently so that the follow-up questionnaire provides reliable information. Don't be haphazard about follow-up. Quality improvements are best made from a consistent database.
13. Know to whom to feed back your follow-up data so that the analysis phase of the instructional system can begin again, with the strength of experience as input. Keep in mind that follow-up requires *responsible action* after the formal follow-up procedure itself is done.

Sample Decisions About the Best Training Delivery Option

The following seven minicases illustrate some actual choices made by training managers about delivering training the most effective way. Together these examples give you an idea of the range of possibilities regarding that piece of "implementation" commonly known as delivery.

The main point is you should always begin by determining exactly what needs to be learned, for which reasons, and exactly by whom. Once you've gotten your objectives and your target audience identified, the delivery mode decision is generally made easier.

Delivering Training According to a Workable and Realistic Schedule

PHCS, the health care management services company, chose to deliver its broad-based training (for example, in customer service and in performance appraisal techniques) in classes lasting no more than two hours. The corporate trainer at PHCS chose this delivery format because two-hour segments are relatively easy to fit into the available time of people who are very preoccupied with growth. In addition, two-hour segments represent the most succinct, most focused, and most necessary training, thereby allowing the trainer to work within the budget even during times of growth. Flexibility and spontaneity are required traits of all managers in a company riding the heady wave of a growth industry; delivering training in two-hour blocks is consistent with this particular corporate culture, and it works for them.

GEER MEMORIAL HEALTH CENTER, a long-term skilled nursing care facility in a competitive and growing personal service industry, designed its basic skill-training program around its philosophy of providing the best possible individualized care. Geer's caregivers don't carry a full patient load for at least four weeks after becoming employed there.

Their training consists of a combination of delivery modes beginning with 24 hours of classroom instruction before they go out onto the patient floors. On the first day on the floor, the trainee works alongside "a super good aide"; on the second day, the trainee handles only one patient, demonstrating the basic skills of lifting, transferring, and bathing; on the third day, the trainee handles two patients. By the end of the first week on the job, the trainee handles three or four patients. Not until at least four weeks of supervised, progressively more demanding on-the-job training tasks have been mastered does the trainee go out on the floor independently.

In contrast to PHCS's short course, Geer's long course stretches over an extended time period. PHCS's training needs are basically for interpersonal, cognitive, or knowledge-based skills; Geer's are for psychomotor skills. Each business developed a training delivery mode and schedule that fit with the objectives for its trainees. Each method of delivering training was workable and acceptable to each business's current corporate culture.

AETNA LIFE AND CASUALTY INSURANCE COMPANY, a large insurance company with typically large numbers of new entry-level employees, had a specific need for these new employees to learn about Aetna's benefits program. The training designer knew that the company was committed to a PC environment for employee information and that this particular benefits information and training program had to be accessible to all kinds of new employees. It also had to be interesting, exploratory, and somewhat playful.

Aetna chose CBT as the delivery mode, and created it for desktop personal computers by using a combination of in-house instructional and graphics designers and external consultants. Aetna believes that the time and expense of development (eight

Continued on page 200

Continued from page 199

to 10 staff members including consultant staff for six to nine months) was worth it because the nature of the content to be learned was individual, personal, and required the learner to explore and choose his or her best options, and because over the course of the training, there would be enough incidences of usage to make its development commitments pay off. In short, this highly accessible, PC-based CBT was the best way to deliver this particular entry-level orientation training. In this case, there was no management-imposed delivery schedule, and, in fact, the delivery of training was initiated by the trainee—an action that was calculated to enhance the learner's readiness to learn. (This CBT program was featured at the May 1991 meeting of the CT Chapter of ASTD, and at the 1991 National Convention of the National Society for Performance and Instruction.)

Delivering Training with Employee Incentives in Mind

BECTON-DICKINSON is the medical supplies manufacturer that's working 24 hours a day. The training administrator has to make training's presence felt equally among all employees—creating equal opportunities for high-quality and consistent training during all shifts, and fulfilling state and federal mandates regarding certification and safety.

This training specialist had to figure out a way to deliver quality training while he wasn't there—he, of course, is working only during the first shift, not during all five shifts. He has developed a mentor-type peer training program featuring Becton-Dickinson's own Subject Matter Experts (SMEs), and he trains employees to be "Task Trainers" using an internally developed train-the-trainer program.

Machine operators are awarded silver certificates for operator certification and gold certificates if selected to be a Task Trainer. Catered award ceremonies are attended by top management. His Task Trainers become skill certified through a skills list audit approach and gain "qualified trainer" status through his train-the-trainer program. The gold certificates are mounted on wood plaques and are displayed in a main corridor in the plant for recognition of achievement.

Trainers are awarded a 10-percent bonus while they are performing their duties as trainers under the supervision of the training administrator, when released by their shift supervisor. Time to be a trainer has been created for each product line when a "floater" employee releases the trainer from production duties when the machines are down for service, when a full complement of workers is present (that is, not out sick), or production schedules let up a little. On-the-job training modules for production employees are continually being developed and certified as technologies or process changes are introduced. Training completions are recorded and tracked via a product line training chart that is prominently displayed in each shift supervisor's office. Quick daily reference to these charts by employees, supervisors, and managers keeps programs on track.

B-D Canaan's technical services specialist says that the program has been a "rewarding success," that attitudes toward training and skill development have improved greatly along with product quality and a sense of commitment by workers. He believes that the recognition of demonstrable skills and incentives for commitment have paid off positively in terms of both human relations and productivity. Worker involvement has enabled him to deliver quality, proactive training with a minimum staff.

Delivering Training Through Cross-Training

CANYON RANCH, "the spa that never leaves you," had to respond to the tremendous challenge of start-up in a complex personal service business that employs many part-time people—two business characteristics that generally are a trainer's nightmare. The managers there embarked upon an ambitious program of cross-training as the delivery mechanism of choice, given the nature of their trainees and their business. In the spa business, a combination of hotel and health services, it's critical that employees know many jobs in order to focus on the individual needs and wants of client-patrons who expect to be treated individually.

Figure 9-4 is an example of the type of checklist that the trainers who are responsible for cross-training at Canyon Ranch use during training. Cross-training is a form of on-the-job training that works very well in meeting the challenges of individualized customer service within complex businesses such as running a spa.

Continued on page 202

Continued from page 201

Figure 9-4. Checklist used by trainers responsible for cross-training at Canyon Ranch.

Kitchen Operations Manual

Training Checklist: Prep Cook   No. E-0062
Prepared by _____   February 10, 19___
Reviewed by _____   Page 1 of 6

I. Orientation
    A. The first 40 hours worked are considered a formal orientation period. The majority of this time is spent with the trainer.
    B. The trainer(s) may be the department head, the supervisor, and/or a co-worker. The trainer is responsible for obtaining answers to any questions the trainee should ask. The trainee is responsible for asking for clarification of anything that is not understood.
    C. It is the responsibility of the trainer to schedule with the trainee a 40-hour plan for the completion of the activities outlined on the Training Checklist below. It is the responsibility of the trainee to give the completed checklist to the department head at the conclusion of the orientation period.

II. Training Checklist

ACTIVITY	SCHEDULED Date/Time	COMPLETED Trainee	Trainer	Date
3. Meet Director of Food Service, Dining Room Manager, Dining Room Assistant Manager and Dining Room Supervisor.	_____	_____	____	____
4. Participate in Hospitality daily guest tour (Clubhouse, daily, 1/2 hour).	_____	_____	____	____
5. Attend Guest Program Orientation (Spa, daily, 1 hour).	_____	_____	____	____
6. Attend benefits orientation (Human Resources, Tuesdays, 3:30 pm, 2 hours).	_____	_____	____	____
7. Complete Skills Inventory (see E-1706).	_____	_____	____	____

Copyright 1989 Canyon Ranch. Reproduced with permission.

Delivering Training at Weekend Retreat

WALLACE COMPANY, INC., Texas-based winner of the 1990 Malcolm Baldrige National Quality Award, got its act together in a very short time, applied for the Baldrige, and won it just three years after it decided to change the way it did business.

Wallace leadership, 280 associates, and the training firm they hired knew that plenty of training had to happen in order for them to satisfy the tough Baldrige criteria. Wallace also knew that finding the time to train all associates in many SPC and human relations skills would be a problem.

Wallace designed the delivery of training around weekend retreats, with full shoulder-to-shoulder participation of the Wallaces themselves and other top leaders. In all, about 19,000 hours of training were delivered—much of it at weekend retreats. It is said that Wallace "reinvented" itself; for them, the retreat format was a training delivery mode that supported those reinvention objectives. (See P. A. Galagan, "How Wallace Changed Its Mind," in *Training and Development,* June 1991.)

Delivering Training During a Week in the Mountains

A downsizing company chose the delivery format of an "outward bound" type program to solidify its values regarding the employees who would be left to carry on a changing business after the reductions in the work force. The vice president in charge of the downsized and restructured work force wanted the message to get out that he valued the individuals who would be asked to survive the change and lead the company forward. He chose the intimate and focused team-building metaphors that wilderness survival is so good at presenting.

Focus on the Issues

These cases illustrate some of the wonderful variety of options that are available to those in charge of making the delivery of training a successful, useful, and cost-effective contributor to business goals.

The simplest and most profound thought about training delivery is that both trainer and trainee alike should abandon the stereotypes that tend to lead them to classroom training in groups of people. The challenge to those in charge of managing training is this:

1. *Take the time to identify* your trainee audience, their learning objectives, and the business factors driving the need for training.

2. *Explore a variety of delivery modes.* Pay attention to both presentation and distribution.
3. *Match up the unique features* of the delivery mode with the special needs of your target audience. Delivery is loaded with process possibilities: Recognize the usefulness of the delivery system itself in moving your trainees closer to improved performance on the job.

More than a Pretty Face and "The Patience of Job"

Many a company has turned an attractive, personable, and patient employee into a trainer. This particular bias for the role of presenter has pervaded training delivery for decades. It also helped fuel the confusion between speech-making and teaching and slowed the acceptance of training-delivery modes that are clearly not instructor-led. Training delivery all too often has not been given its full value as a critical part of the instructional system.

But times are changing. As work becomes more computer-intensive, we have more reasons and opportunities to use the computer and all forms of information technology for learning in the context of work. Savvy training managers look not only for ways to minimize overhead but also for ways to reduce the learning cycle.

The important thing to remember is that today there are numerous well-developed possibilities for delivering training to a wide variety of employees. Your major task as training manager is to keep your mind alert, your options open, and your biases quiet. Good delivery demands that good research and development precede it.

Chapter 10

Performance and Evaluation

Finally, we address in a specific way the related issues of performance and evaluation as we understand the interrelationship in today's changing training scene. Enterprises of all sorts and sizes are defining ways to morph training into the larger idea of performance, and the results of training experiences are figuring into bigger corporate goals. Training can no longer be viewed as an end in itself, engaged in and evaluated for its value as a learning experience. Employee development—the second part of the traditional "training and development"—is viewed today as a business responsibility from both a personal or individual point of view and a corporate perspective. What happens during and as a result of training, as well as the "developed" employee's worth to a company, today is viewed through the performance lens. It's no longer enough for individuals to be good students in class and for companies to offer well-designed courses taught by excellent instructors. Better performance of individuals and better performance of the processes by which they work feed better organizational and corporate performance. Performance is the foundation for business and personal growth.

> "The Stop & Shop Supermarket Company strives to employ the best qualified people, to provide equal opportunities for the advancement of employees, including promotion and training, and to administer these activities in a manner that will not discriminate against any person because of race, color, religion, sex, age, national origin, marital status, disability, sexual orientation or any other characteristic protected by law."

Training with a Focus on Performance

To illustrate what performance is all about, we've chosen to feature Customer Service training at the Super Stop & Shop supermarket in Winsted, Connecticut. We start with Stop & Shop's application form, an excerpt from which is reproduced in the box above.

Notice that the store is looking for qualified people—"the best qualified" people—that they strive to provide for equal opportunities for advancement—"including promotion and training." These phrases contain the most basic elements of performance in them: qualifications, opportunities, and the motivation for improvement that comes with promotion and learning. Right away, you can see that *performance*—of the individual, the work processes at this store, and the store as a whole—is written into the framework of this mission statement on the application form.

The Winsted Super Stop & Shop is the market where I do my grocery shopping. True to its broad statement of non-discrimination, this store hires and trains qualified adults with mental handicaps as customer service clerks. These men and women are on the frontline of customer service performing the important work of bagging the customer's order, loading it into the shopping cart, and sending customers on their way with a smile. Betty Begin, head of the Customer Service Department at the store, said that she has hired persons with mental disabilities off the street, from referrals of peers and colleagues, and from referrals from agencies such as Easter Seals, the Kennedy Center, and local associations who advocate for handicapped adults. She has placed and trained persons with mental retardation, with permanent effects of rehabilitated substance abuse, and with physical handicaps. She says that these customer service clerks are outstanding because of their positive attitudes, reliability, punctuality, dependability, and motivation.

The landmark Americans with Disabilities Act (ADA), Public Law 101-336, was signed into law by President George Bush on July 26, 1990, in an elaborate ceremony in the White House Rose Garden. It applies to employers with 15 or more workers. In addition to coverage of persons with physical disabilities, the law covers persons with mental disabilities including stress and depression attributable to a clinically diagnosed mental disorder; persons with learning disabilities such as dyslexia; persons with psychosis; and persons with mental retardation. To be covered under the employment provisions of ADA regarding mental disabilities, a job applicant must provide prospective employers with a record of having been previously diagnosed or classified as an individual with mental impairment (American Management Association's "Special Report ADA IN ACTION" in *HR Focus* newsletter, 1992, p.8). Tool 1, discussed later in this chapter, contains more detail on ADA.

Legal talk can sound complicated to an employer, so we return to Betty Begin and her customer service clerks at Super Stop & Shop to put a human face on issues of performance. The first important issue in performance is competence and its legal counterpart, "qualification." That is, is an employee competent to perform work and is he or she qualified for the job that needs to be performed? The issue of competence comes before training; it needs to be assessed before an individual is matched up with a job and before training ever enters the picture. Competence can include physical characteristics such as speed and accuracy of response to stimulus, strength, and ability to repeat patterns of behavior; intellectual characteristics such as ability to learn from one's mistakes, ability to deal with ambiguity, and ability to make decisions; emotional characteristics such as willingness to share, assertiveness, and respect for others; and such attitudinal characteristics as loyalty, courage, and trustworthiness. Jobs require *competent* individuals.

Jobs also require that persons who hold them are qualified to do the many tasks that the job entails. This means that persons applying for a job are entitled to know just what those qualifications are. Employers have a responsibility to determine what jobs require, and to specify those requirements in the form of qualifications. The competencies required for a specific job must be spelled out as qualifications, written down, publicized, and circulated to all persons equally. The ADA, as one example of legislation, makes it very clear that employers are legally responsible for accurately stating job qualifications.

As Stop & Shop says, it "strives to employ the *best qualified people.*" The Stop & Shop Supermarket Company in Winsted, Connecticut, is part of a huge supermarket conglomerate corporation, Royal Ahold of The Netherlands. This corporation is the eleventh largest such company in the world, and it owns markets in Europe, South America, Asia, and the United States, with new stores opening worldwide. Bi-Lo, Edwards/Giant (Carlisle, PA), Giant (Landover, MD), and TOPS/Finast are "sister" companies across the U.S. related to my Super Stop & Shop in Winsted. There are 69 Stop & Shop Supermarkets in the state of Connecticut alone, and 193 markets chainwide. This defines a very large employee market. Stop & Shop's Centralized Training Division Coordinator, Wally Beach, said that Stop & Shop has very extensive job descriptions that spell out the tasks required of anyone in that job. The notion of qualifications as both an employer responsibility and an employee responsibility helps the reader focus on the idea of performance. Without qualified employees, jobs don't get done. Without qualified employees, training doesn't make sense, is a waste of resources, and is rightfully questioned about its reason for being. The *performance* contract between employer and employee, before training ever enters the equation, requires both parties to responsibly represent job qualifications.

Stop & Shop's mission statement also says that the company strives "to provide equal opportunities for the advancement of employees, including promotion and training." The two ideas joined here—the idea of equal opportunities and the idea of promotion and training—are also key ideas to an understanding of performance and training's role in it. In the case of the Winsted Super Stop & Shop's customer service clerks, opportunities abound for promotion based on performance, consistent with union requirements. Begin's customer service clerks look forward to promotions to other departments such as grocery, produce, deli, or bake shop, and to jobs beyond bagging groceries, such as packaging, stacking produce, "panning up" in the bake shop, and taking care of bottle returns. Like bagging customers' orders, these jobs require skill, decision making, and positive work attitudes, as well as good performance of the many tasks associated with them.

Stop & Shop has an incentive program too, beyond the incentive for promotion. Stop & Shop employees are eligible for "Way To Go!" cards as compliments for excellent performance on the job. Both instant recognition and long-term recognition can earn an employee a "Way To Go!" card. Cards are accumulated and traded in for merchandise that employees select from an awards catalog. Tools, electronics, and household products are some of the choices. The "Store Management Team" (whose 8-x-10-inch photos are posted at the customer service desk) has a letter on the inside cover of the awards catalog that says:

> Your outstanding performance has earned you Stop
> & Shop Recognition Award Points .... Your perform-
> ance and commitment to service, quality, and
> excellence is what makes Stop & Shop the top
> choice of our customers. We know it's associates
> like you that bring our customers back, time and
> time again! Best wishes for continued success and
> thanks again for a job well done!

Motivation, incentives, recognition—all these are critical elements of high performance. I am one of the customers who comes back time and time again. Curious about the training of the Winsted store's customer service clerks, I spent some time wandering around the store watching some on-the-job training and supervision by various managers. Supervisors carefully talk with and monitor the service clerks, making sure that each one stays focused on the tasks at hand and interacts with customers in a cheerful way. With so many people walking back and forth in a large supermarket, it is not immediately apparent that on-the-job training is happening. When I asked Begin how this works, she said, "I watch them, remind them, help them out, get them back on track, and cover for them if it looks like a bad day." ADA might call some of this "reasonable accommodation" to the key processes of a person's job; others might call it good supervision, an example of good leadership, or just plain on-the-job training. Job performance is the goal; training is a means to accomplish that goal.

ADA might also consider Stop & Shop's approach an admirable example of a coherent performance-focused program aimed at full integration of individuals with disabilities into the rhythm of work at a supermarket. Stop & Shop has centralized training for new hires from a group of stores. This training is surely an opportunity of employment, and is engaged in by all new hires. Betty's customer service clerks train side by side with new employees from other stores in this particular region of the state of Connecticut. After classroom training in company policies and practices by a centralized training staff, new hires attend specialized departmental training in a working supermarket. This is hands-on training with real colleagues and real customers in the skills and knowledge requirements of the department in which the new hire will be placed back at the home store. In the case of the customer service clerks, they are trained in how to bag groceries, how to handle spills, what to do about returns, how to interact with customers, and how to deal with shopping carriages. Wally Beach, spokesman for the centralized training operation, notes that Stop & Shop is dedicated to providing accommodation during training for individuals with special needs. That is, if a trainee has a hearing loss, Stop & Shop provides an interpreter or sign language specialist; if a trainee has a learning disability, a job coach is made available during training. The secret to the Stop & Shop success is the individual accommodation approach, *especially during training*.

Local stores identify trainers from among the management staff or the associate staff at large who receive train-the-trainer training at the centralized training facility. Stop & Shop's training is focused on performance, and recognizes that training is just one element of the complex picture that is excellence in customer service. Wally Beach also comments that Stop & Shop chose to assure quality in training of new hires by responding to customer demands and the changing nature of market trends. In Connecticut, as elsewhere in the country, supermarket stores have been getting bigger in recent years, with a growing need for part-time workers to accommodate expanded store hours. Customers want more departments and one-stop-shopping for the necessities of complex daily living; and more people want to work part-time. All in all, the changing customer and workplace trends called for a *training change*—away from decentralized catch-as-catch-can training in local stores to coordinated, standardized training in a central location. In the case of this business, centralized training became the answer to controlling the new market variables, and it also becomes a model of equal opportunity in a core operational function of the supermarket, customer service.

Performance Essentials

An earlier section of this book introduced the classic "performance technology" model developed by Thomas F. Gilbert 20 years ago. He called his model of human performance "The Behavior Engineering Model." His book, which is generally credited with starting the "performance" movement in earnest, is titled *Human Competence: Engineering Worthy Performance,* a title that contains the essential ideas that human performance depends upon things that an individual can do to improve, as well as things that an individual's environment (family, school, work, community) can do to improve. Within this representation, training, or as Gilbert says, "scientifically designed training that matches the requirements of exemplary performance," is only one of 16 essential factors for excellent performance. Gilbert's original model is reproduced as Figure 10-1.

Figure 10-1. Gilbert's Behavior Engineering Model.

The Behavior Engineering Model

	S^0 Information	R Instrumentation	S_r Motivation
E **Environmental** **supports**	**Data** 1. Relevant and frequent feedback about the adequacy of performance 2. Descriptions of what is expected of performance 3. Clear and relevant guides to adequate performance	**Instruments** 1. Tools and materials of work designed scientifically to match human factors	**Incentives** 1. Adequate financial incentives made contingent upon performance 2. Nonmonetary incentives made available 3. Career-development opportunities
P **Person's** **repertory of** **behavior**	**Knowledge** 1. Scientifically designed training that matches the requirements of exemplary performance 2. Placement	**Capacity** 1. Flexible scheduling of performance to match peak capacity 2. Prosthesis 3. Physical shaping 4. Adaptation 5. Selection	**Motives** 1. Assessment of people's motives to work 2. Recruitment of people to match the realities of the situation

Source: From Thomas F. Gilbert, *Human Competence: Engineering Worthy Performance.* New York: McGraw-Hill, 1978, p. 88. Reproduced with permission of the International Society for Performance Improvement (ISPI), which now owns the copyright, 1996.

In addition to the paradigm shift away from training for training's sake and the notion of human behavior's worth or value, Gilbert pointed out that other factors besides training are necessary "engineering" components in building better behavior. These include data and information, tools and materials with which to perform work, non-monetary incentives and career development opportunities, recruitment for and placement in the right job, a person's store of acquired knowledge and skills, one's innate capacity or competency, and a person's need to work and motivation for working. These ideas have spawned a human performance technology movement, numerous publications and organizations devoted to classifying and representing human performance, and a recognition on the part of trainers that performance improvement is the framework within which training is one of many contributors. In fact, letterhead of ASTD, now carries these words: "Delivering Performance in a Changing World."

ASTD itself, through the work of William Rothwell, has adapted Thomas Gilbert's behavior engineering model as a representation of how to figure out the cause(s) of poor performance. ASTD's human performance analysis model is reproduced in Figure 10-2.

Figure 10-2. Fishbone diagram to analyze cause(s) of human performance gaps.

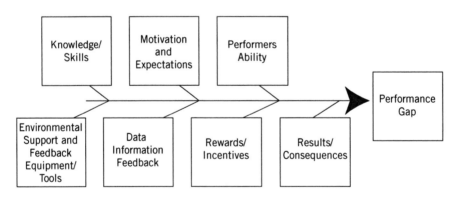

This model is adapted from Thomas Gilbert's Behavioral Engineering Model.

Source: From William J. Rothwell, *ASTD Models for Human Performance Improvement: Roles, Competencies, and Outputs.* Alexandria,VA: American Society for Training & Development, 1996, p. 14. Reprinted with permission.

With these models in mind, we return to the Winsted Super Stop & Shop supermarket. It's easy to see that Stop & Shop is getting it right when it comes to "engineering" good performance from its customer service clerks. Store management clearly pays attention to both the "environmental supports" provided by the company and the individual's behaviors that lead to success on the job. Stop & Shop pays attention to information, instrumentation, and motivation at both the company and the personal levels. When performance "gaps" occur, you can be sure that the management team knows that there are places other than training to look for causes. Stop & Shop's centralized training is right on the money when it trained local store managers and others to be trainers—to provide just-in-time and just-enough training to increase the value of on-the-job performance when it can make the most difference to customer satisfaction. Tool 2, discussed later, suggests some of the differences between training and performance; it can be helpful to you as you move from training to performance. Trainers who see their training mission in the broader context of performance will have an easier time of choosing the right training for the right reasons for the right people—in short, of rising to the quality challenge of getting it right the first time. Stop & Shop's motto is "Service, Quality, Excellence."

Evaluation's Triple Focus

The idea of a performance gap introduces the role of evaluation in the performance system. Like training needs assessment, performance needs assessment is a process of determining what standards need to be met for performance to be good, and, likewise, what standards are not being met when performance is bad. Evaluative processes such as monitoring, pre- and post-testing, working against a checklist, 360-degree feedback, and performance review are fundamental to making improvements in the way people, processes, and entire organizations perform. "What should be versus what is" rings true for an approach for both trainers and performance specialists. Like training needs assessment, performance needs assessment is seen as the beginning of a developmental system, and evaluation is seen as the system's end stage. In both cases, feedback at all stages of system development is critical to effective system performance. System interrelationships are important. Knowing where to look for data that will yield results useful to your business is the secret. The broad view of performance technology, with training as only one part of it, is the right mind-set.

Evaluation in any human development system should have a triple focus: on the individual, the process, and the organization. In terms of a performance improvement program, an individual's job performance should be evaluated, the various processes and procedures of his or her work should be evaluated for how well they support personal effort and encourage success, and the performance of the organization as a whole should be evaluated according to its business mission and its indices for excellence. Tool 3 (see later discussion) presents the widely accepted Kirkpatrick Four Levels of Evaluation, an evaluation model that views training within a larger performance system. ASTD's "1999 State of the Industry Report" noted that by the year 2000, the high-performing companies surveyed in the study—companies in the ASTD Benchmarking Forum—expect to evaluate training at these levels:

Level 1 (reaction):	79 percent of companies
Level 2 (learning):	45 percent of companies
Level 3 (behavior):	27 percent of companies
Level 4 (results):	17 percent of companies

Similar studies by other organizations that focus on human resources note similar trends: it is hard work and resource-intensive to evaluate the results of improved performance. The good news is that companies that are considered leaders in their fields are making a greater commitment to tie training and performance to business growth. The important thing to remember is that the reasons for good performance are found in many different but related places, and that as training becomes a key to successful performance and not an end in itself, the business reasons for evaluation put more pressure on trainers to evaluate the entire spectrum of work performance—individual, process, and organization. Tool 4 suggests ways to think about measurement; Tool 5 lists some of the key factors in the business costs associated with poor performance. (Tools are discussed later. See Box 10-1 for summary.)

What Evaluation Can Do for You

Perhaps the most famous example of evaluation in American business is the process of applying for the Malcolm Baldrige National Quality Award, presented annually since 1987 by the National Institute of Standards and Technology of the U.S. Department of Commerce. "The Baldrige," as it is commonly known, is committed to challenging American companies to build quality into their daily routines so that business results will be positively affected as a result of conscious efforts at many levels. It is an example of what evaluation can do for your company, no matter what your size.

The 1998 set of guidelines, or "criteria," for The Baldrige featured a new title, *The 1998 Criteria for Performance Excellence*. A cover letter with the criteria booklet from the program's director, Harry S. Hertz, said, "Increased focus has been given to all aspects of organizational and employee learning," and "the 1998 criteria further strengthen the systems view of performance management and place a greater emphasis on the alignment of company strategy, customer and market knowledge, a high-performance work force, key company processes, and business results."

These statements, too, suggest the importance of the individual, the process, and the organization. The Baldrige criteria for excellent performance are organized into seven groups, with points awarded by an evaluating team. The seven groups are:

- Leadership
- Strategic Planning
- Customer and Market Focus
- Information and Analysis
- Human Resource Focus
- Process Management
- Business Results

A total of 1,000 points is possible. Out of the seven categories, by far the weightiest category is "Business Results: Performance results, trends, and comparison to competitors in key business areas—customer satisfaction, financial and marketplace, human resources, suppliers and partners, and operations," worth 450 points. If you're looking for guidance in how to develop a "taxonomy" of performance, The Baldrige is a good place to start. (Get more information from the American Society for Quality [ASQ], which administers the award, Milwaukee, Wisconsin, 800.248.1946; or from the National Institute of Standards and Technology, Gaithersburg, Maryland, 301.975.2036.)

Working toward achieving performance excellence in categories of The Baldrige can help you design and deliver your training so that it is part of a performance system focused on business results. The Baldrige Criteria is reproduced in Figure 10-3. Whether or not you ever apply for the award, it's worth using the criteria booklet as a guide to better performance at all levels of corporate structure.

Figure 10-3. The Baldrige criteria.

Instructions: Refer to this chart to study how these criteria are grouped to lead to "performance excellence" or to lead your organization forward to request for information about "The Baldrige" from ASQ or the Department of Commerce. One thousand points represent 100 percent; the numerator indicates the point value for each category.

Leadership: The company's leadership system, values, expectations, and public responsibilities.   110/1000

    Leadership System   (80)

    Company Responsibility and Citizenship   (30)

Strategic Planning: The effectiveness of strategic and business planning and deployment of plan, with a strong focus on customer and operational performance requirements.   80/1000

    Strategy Development Process   (40)

    Company Strategy   (40)

Customer and Market Focus: How the company determines customer and market requirements and expectations, enhances relationships and customers, and determines their satisfaction.   80/1000

    Customer and Market Knowledge   (40)

    Customer Satisfaction and Relationship Enhancement   (40)

Information and Analysis: The effectiveness of information collection and analysis to support customer-driven performance excellence and marketplace success.   80/1000

    Selection and Use of Information and Data   (25)

    Selection and Use of Comparative Information and Data   (15)

    Analysis and Review of Company Performance   (40)

Human Resource Focus: The success of efforts to realize the full potential of the work force to create a high-performance organization.   100/1000

    Work Systems   (40)

    Employee Education, Training, & Development   (30)

    Employee Well-Being and Satisfaction   (30)

Process Management: The effectiveness of systems and
processes for assuring the quality of products and services. 100/1000
    Management of Product & Service Processes (60)
    Management of Support Processes (20)
    Management of Supplier and Partnering Processes (20)

Business Results: Performance results, trends,
and comparison to competitors in key business
areas—customer satisfaction, financial and
marketplace, human resources, suppliers and
partners, and operations. 450/1000
    Customer Satisfaction Results (125)
    Financial and Market Results (125)
    Human Resource Results (50)
    Supplier and Partner Results (25)
    Company-Specific Results (125)

Source: From *The 1998 Criteria for Performance Excellence*, p.2, and *1998 Application Forms and Instructions*, p.2.

Box10-1. Tools for performance and evaluation.

1. *Primer on the Americans with Disabilities Act (ADA)*—A list of the key provisions of this important piece of federal legislation that support both employers and employees in their efforts to hire, place, train, and develop persons with disabilities into high performers

2. *Training Versus Performance*—A chart and a model illustrating differences between traditional training and performance, showing clear relationships between the training system and the performance system, and indicating where training fits as a key component of a performance system

3. *Four Levels of Evaluation*—A definition of Kirkpatrick's Four Levels of Evaluation, generally accepted as a representation of the evaluation processes that are necessary in showing correlations and causation in the development of human resources to support business results

4. *Ways to Think about Measurement*—A list of measurement variables to spark your imagination as you plan the monitoring and evaluation of individuals, processes, and organizations

5. *Costs of Poor Performance*—A chart defining the most common costs of poor performance

Tool 1. Primer on the Americans with Disabilities Act (ADA), PL 101-336

One of the major purposes of the ADA is to make it easier for persons with disabilities to get and hold jobs, and to have the equal

---

advantage of having accessible public services and facilities. The ADA's employment provisions have been gradually phased in, with the last phase-in of small businesses on July 26, 1994. As of that date, the law covers employers with 15 to 24 employees. Organizations with fewer than 15 employees are exempt from the employment discrimination requirements of ADA. New challenges to ADA are periodically litigated, and the Supreme Court is sometimes requested to make new interpretations of the law. Check with your senator or congressperson for information about the latest information. Keep in mind that ADA's purpose, from its beginning and now, is to ensure access to equal employment opportunities based on merit. The last U.S. Census indicated that approximately 17 percent of the American population has a physical or mental impairment ("Special Report: ADA IN ACTION," in *HR Focus,* New York: American Management Association, 1992, p. 15). Guaranteeing equal opportunity to all citizens is an inviolable foundation of our government, and the reason so many of us enjoy the benefits of employment.

- *Individuals Protected by ADA.* Three basic categories are specified:
  1. Any individual with a physical or mental impairment that substantially limits one or more major life activities
  2. Anyone with a record of such impairment
  3. Anyone regarded as having such an impairment
- *Reasonable Accommodation.* When an individual's disability creates a barrier to employment opportunities, ADA requires employers to consider whether reasonable accommodation(s) could remove the barrier. Employers, employment agencies, labor organizations, and joint labor-management committees under ADA must "make reasonable accommodation to the known limitations of a qualified applicant or employee unless to do so would cause an undue hardship" (*The President's Committee on Employment of People with Disabilities Fact Sheet on The Americans with Disabilities Act, Public Law 101-336,* Washington, DC: Bureau of National Affairs, 1992, p. 1). Accommodations fall into these categories: to the job application process, to the work environment, to job procedures, and to other benefits and privileges of employment (*The Supervisor's Guide to the Americans with Disabilities Act,* Bureau of Business Practice, Simon & Schuster, 1993, p. 10). These are some typical reasonable accommodations regarding jobs and working:

1. Restructuring a job by reallocating or redistributing marginal job functions
2. Altering when or how an essential job function is performed
3. Providing part-time or modified work schedules
4. Obtaining devices that provide assistance
5. Modifying equipment
6. Modifying training materials, examinations, and policies
7. Providing a job coach, aide, reader, or interpreter
8. Reassignment to a vacant position
9. Providing reserved parking near an individual's workstation

- *Qualifications.* A qualified individual with disabilities is one who can perform the essential functions of a job with or without reasonable accommodation.
- *Tax Credits and Financial Assistance to Employers.* The Federal government provides financial assistance to employers regarding their good faith reasonable accommodation efforts. (Dollars and language quoted here are from the publication, *The Americans with Disabilities Act: Access and Accommodations* by Nancy Hablutzel and Brian T. McMahon, Boca Raton, FL: St. Lucie Press, 1998, pp. III-35-36. Check with your congressional representative for updated information. Regional ADA Technical Assistance Offices are scattered throughout the U.S. as a resource for employers and others implementing ADA.)
  1. *Tax Credit for Small Business, Section 44 of the Internal Revenue Code.* An eligible small business is one with gross receipts of $1 million or less for the taxable year, or with 30 or fewer full-time employees. An eligible small business may take a tax credit of up to $5,000 per year for accommodations made to comply with ADA. The U.S. Department of Justice can provide publications about the ADA and small businesses, along with periodic status reports of new interpretations and provisions of ADA. (Telephone the DOJ at 800.514.0301.)
  2. *Tax Deduction for Removal of Architectural and Transportation Barriers, Section 190 of the Internal Revenue Code.* Any business may take a tax deduction, up to $15,000 per year, for removal of such barriers.

3. *Targeted Jobs Tax Credit (TJTCP)*. Tax credits are available for employers who hire individuals with disabilities referred by state or local vocational rehabilitation agencies, State Commissions on the Blind, and the U.S. Department of Veterans Affairs and certified by a State Employment Service. Check with your congressional office to get the latest information regarding efforts at federal jobs program consolidation legislation. As of 1998, under TJTCP, an employer may take a tax credit equal to 40 percent of the first $6,000 of an eligible employee's salary. Other similar state and local funding sources may be available.

4. *Preferred Language and Expression Regarding ADA.* Those complying with ADA soon find themselves changing their vocabulary. The first thing to notice is the language of the title of PL 101-336: The Americans *with* Disabilities Act. The language throughout ADA encourages readers to refer to persons for whom the law was enacted as individuals or persons *with* something, not persons who are without something. The following chart provides a few examples; focus on the use of the word "with":

negative	positive
the disabled	people with disabilities
a retarded person	person with mental retardation
deformed, crippled, defective	person with a disability
confined to a wheelchair	person who uses a wheelchair
lame, maimed, withered	walks with a limp
Mongoloid	person with Down's syndrome
former mental patient, deviant	person with mental illness
hunchback	person with spinal curvature
brain-damaged	person with a head injury

Tool 2. Training Versus Performance

The chart below suggests some of the most common differences between a focus on training alone versus a focus on performance. It can be helpful to you as you begin to see how to structure and deliver the best possible training within the best possible performance system.

training	performance
event-focused	process-focused
reactive and responsive	proactive and responsive

evaluates learning	evaluates impact of performance
often happens in isolation	must have organizational connections
focused on what a person needs to learn	focused on what a person needs to do

Figure 10-3 is the ASTD model of Performance Technology. It was developed by ASTD, with credit to W.A. Deterline and M.J. Rosenberg of the International Society for Performance Improvement (ISPI). Notice in this reproduction that the training function, or "Skills and Knowledge," is highlighted to indicate that it is only one part of the broader and more complex performance system.

Figure 10-3. A performance technology model.

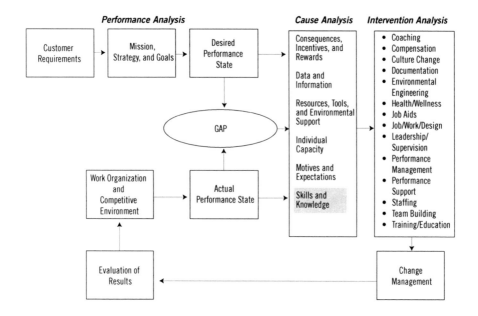

Source: From W.A. Deterline and M.J. Rosenberg, *Workplace Productivity: Performance Technology Success Stories,* Washington, DC: the International Society for Performance Improvement, 1992. It is reprinted here from William J. Rothwell's *ASTD Models for Human Performance Improvement,* Alexandria, VA: American Society for Training & Development, 1996, p. 7.

Tool 3. Levels of Evaluation

Donald L. Kirkpatrick, professor emeritus at University of Wisconsin, is a former national president of the American Society for Training & Development and still a presence at ASTD's annual international conference, where his sessions on "The Four Levels" of evaluation are well attended. Kirkpatrick codified his ideas about training evaluation in a book, *Evaluating Training Programs: The Four Levels,* published by Berrett-Koehler in 1994. This book reflects Kirkpatrick's 40 years of involvement in the ideas and practices of training evaluation and is still a well-read classic in the field. His was among the first voices calling for a broader and deeper perspective on the evaluation of training. Like today's performance technologists, he saw the role of training in corporate success as broader than what happened in corporate classrooms.

In the early pages of his book, Kirkpatrick talks about the reasons why we need to evaluate training, and summarizes them this way: we need to evaluate training to justify the existence of the training department in relationship to the larger corporate goals, to provide us with information about whether to continue or discontinue or modify certain training programs or courses, and to provide us with information on making future improvements to the training operation and specific programs in it (p. 18). Kirkpatrick also points out early in his book (p. 20) that wise trainers will evaluate at all four levels and communicate the results to top management.

These are Kirkpatrick's Four Levels:

1. *Reaction.* Reaction of trainees to a particular training experience or event. Most often measured at the conclusion of a seminar or course. Questions generally include the trainee's reaction to the training room, the materials, the instructor's presentation skills, the organization of content, the schedule, and even the refreshments. Often referred to as the "smiles sheet." Sometimes considered a measure of "customer satisfaction" with the training process.

2. *Learning.* Focused on a demonstrated change in behavior as a result of a training experience. Often evaluated by pre- and post-tests that show an increase in knowledge, improvement in skill, or a positive attitude change. Online measurement of learning can facilitate pre- and post-testing. Focused on the content of training and a trainee's understanding of it as demonstrated by positive behavior change. Generally thought of as the province of the K, S, As—knowledge, skills, and attitudes. Generally reserved for the learning that can be documented immediately before and immediately after the "intervention" of training. This kind of evaluation often measures whether or not the objectives of the training have been met.

3. *Behavior.* Evaluation of the application of what was taught and learned during training. A focus on changes in the trainee's behavior or way of doing things back on the job. Hard to measure because success depends on factors outside of knowledge, skills, and attitudes developed during training. Changed behavior also requires motivation, a favorable working environment, incentives, and rewards. Difficult to attribute on-the-job success to training alone.

4. *Results.* Impact of specific training on business results, such as increased sales, decreased costs, fewer errors, reduced turnover, fewer accidents, increased production, wider margins, higher profits, better return on investment. The most difficult to evaluate and show causality. Many evaluators today are suggesting that showing correlation is sufficient, and that trainers need to focus diligently on doing that.

Kirkpatrick has long advocated evaluating training programs at all four levels because he believes that levels one and two give trainers the opportunity to gain enthusiasm, confidence to talk business at higher levels, and some good data as a foundation for levels three and four. His 1994 book belongs in every training manager's library of resources. The message is clear: Show what training does best, and then take it to higher levels of influence.

Tool 4. Ways to Think about Measurement

Perhaps the first thing to ask yourself when you decide to "take measurements" of a process or of an individual's performance is what the results will be used for—that is, ask yourself *utility* questions. What is the usefulness of this measure? Why do I want to measure this? What good business reasons can I list for doing this measurement? Answering the usefulness question first will help you get your head straight about what to measure. Never test or measure for its own sake; that can get you into legal trouble. Measurements need to be designed carefully with questions of fairness always at the forefront. Measurements need to specifically, obviously, clearly relate to a business purpose. Here are some other variables to consider as you plan measurement activities:

- *Focus:* The more narrow, the better. Zero in on your objective and develop measurements that capture only that objective. Don't confuse people with extraneous information. Don't measure the wrong things.

- *Performance standards:* Find current, consistent standards. Find these in the language of job descriptions, piece-work targets, by watching outstanding performers and taking notes, training documents (learning objectives, skills lists, checklists), past practices that have been rewarded, sales records, safety records, etc. Make a coherent set of standards if you don't already have one. Don't engage in measurement activities until all persons to be measured have had a reasonable opportunity to know what the standards are and have had a reasonable amount of time to demonstrate on the job that they can work toward achieving the specified standards. Never play "I gotcha" with measurement. Respect the fact that most people at work want to do a good job and deserve the opportunity to show that they can perform acceptably.
- *Obstacles:* Remove the obstacles. Look around and find out what the obstacles to measurement are in your company. Is the time and place right for measurement activities? Can you incorporate measurement into the normal flow of work so that it doesn't become something "other than" work? Do you have the right materials and instruments to measure what you need to measure? Do walls, buildings, schedules get in the way of effective measurement practices? Are the people you need to be involved available and ready to engage in measurement?
- *Feedback:* If you can convince your employees that evaluation is a critical part of building the capacity to learn and to make continuous improvements in performance, you can use the process of measurement and its results profitably. If you're in charge of training, no matter what your title is, you need to convey the message to those around you that feedback is the lifeblood of any system. Those who participate in measurement and evaluation are entitled to the results. They are also entitled to a voice in making changes based on the results. Those giving and receiving feedback all need to enter into the feedback process with the same goal: to improve performance. Feedback should not be allowed to degenerate into personalized criticisms, nor should it be allowed to be so general that it's useless. Do not enter into feedback sessions unprepared; have all relevant data at hand, share it, and focus on the data and its uses. Be

prepared psychologically, too, to respect all persons' points of view and their need for a safe environment to give and receive feedback. Feedback is a learning process.

Tool 5. Costs of Poor Performance

Poor performance of individuals and of processes costs the organization—and company—many kinds of things. When you think about the findings of the various things you have measured, you soon see that numbers can be assigned to your findings, numbers such as percent, sum, time, frequency, range, and dollars. The chart below suggests ways to look at various kinds of costs associated with poor performance of work processes and of individual workers. Assigning appropriate numbers to any of these kinds of items, after measurement, can help you determine the costs of poor performance, and, likewise, provide motivation for change:

Work Systems	Quality	Employee Well-Being and Satisfaction
items sold	amount of waste	cost of grievances
items inventoried	number of errors	cost of litigation
items produced	number of rejects	days absent
items processed	hours to rework	rate of turnover
customers served		cost of misinformation
		cost of accidents

Training in the Context of Performance

Tools in this chapter on performance and evaluation can lead you into structuring your training operation, big or small, around the important ideas that working is about doing—about performance. Working in American companies is also about equal opportunity, empowerment, and the sharing of corporate values and successes. Training must be designed and delivered to support performance of individuals and of work processes, and to support organizational viability. Knowledge, skills, and work attitudes are the province of training. Seeing your training operation in the larger context of performance, and using the powers of evaluation to guide positive change, is a good place to start. The real people with real training challenges featured in this book can provide you with some guidance and motivation to create your own high-performing training operation.

Bibliography

American Management Association (AMA). *HRfocus: Special Report ADA IN ACTION.* New York: 1992.

American Society for Training & Development (ASTD). *Training America: Learning to Work in the 21st Century.* Alexandria, VA: 1989.

_____, *National Report on Human Resources.* Alexandria, VA: October 1990.

_____, "News & Trends." *Technical & Skills Training.* Alexandria, VA: January 1991.

_____, *Training Benchmarking Report,* 1997. Alexandria, VA: October 1997.

Bassi, Laurie J. and Mark E. Van Buren. "The 1999 State of the Industry Report." *Training & Development,* January 1999.

Bloom, B. S. *Taxonomy of Educational Objectives. Book 1: Cognitive Domain.* New York: Longmans, 1954.

Bureau of Business Practice. *The Supervisor's Guide to the Americans with Disabilities Act.* Waterford, CT: 1993.

Bureau of National Affairs (BNA). *BNA's Americans with Disabilities Act Manual.* Washington, DC: 1992.

Bureau of National Affairs. *The President's Committee on Employment of People with Disabilities Factsheet on the Americans with Disabilities Act, Public Law 101-336.* Washington, DC: 1992

Carnevale, A. P. "America and the New Economy." *Training & Development Journal,* November 1990.

Chang , R. V. *An Introduction to Human Resource Development Careers.* 3rd ed. Alexandria, VA: American Society for Training & Development, September 1990.

Cohen, Sacha. "Big Ideas for Trainers in Small Companies" in *Training & Development,* April 1998.

Deming, W. E. *Quality, Productivity and Competitive Position.* Cambridge, MA: MIT Center for Advanced Engineering Study, 1982.

Dun & Bradstreet. *The Challenge of Managing a Small Business.* Murray Hill, NJ: 1989.

Ellis, Ryann. "The Nuts and Bolts" sidebar within N. Kuhn "Training from Scratch" in *Training & Development,* October 1998.

Fuhrman, P. "Soviet Generals to Gorbachev: We Are Defenseless." *Forbes,* April 1, 1991.

Galagan, P. A. "How Wallace Changed Its Mind." *Training & Development Journal,* June 1991.

Ganzel, Rebecca. "Winner Take All" training salary survey in *Training,* November 1997.

Geber, B. "Budgets Barely Budge." *Training,* October 1990.

Gilbert, T. F. *Human Competence: Engineering Worthy Performance.* New York: McGraw-Hill, 1978.

Guba, E. G. and Y. S. Lincoln. *Effective Evaluation.* San Francisco: Jossey-Bass, 1981.

Hoover, C. W. Jr. "Return on Investment in Engineering Education." *Proceedings* of the Sixth IEEE-USA Careers Conference. New York: Institute of Electrical and Electronics Engineers.

Hablutzel, Nancy and Brian T. McMahon. *The Americans with Disabilities Act: Access and Accommodations.* Boca Raton, FL: St. Lucie Press LLC, 1998.

Horton, M. "Wallace Goes for the Baldrige." *Supply House Times,* October 1990.

Hudson Institute. *Workforce 2000: Work and Workers for the 21st Century.* W. B. Johnston, Project Director, and A. H. Packer, Co-Project Director. Indianapolis, IN: 1987.

_____, *Workforce 2020: Work and Workers in the 21st Century.* Richard W. Judy, Senior Research Fellow, and Carol D'Amico, Project Director and Senior Research Fellow. Indianapolis, IN: 1997.

IBM Annual Report—1990.

"IBM, A Special Company." *Think Magazine,* September 1989.

Kirkpatrick, Donald L. *Evaluating Training Programs: The Four Levels.* San Francisco: Berrett-Koehler, 1994.

Knowles, M. H. *The Adult Learner, A Neglected Species.* 3rd ed. Houston: Gulf Publishing Co., 1984.

Krathwohl, D. R., B. S. Bloom, and B. B. Masia. *Taxonomy of Educational Objectives. Book 2: Affective Domain.* New York: Longmans, 1964.

Lammers, T. "How to Spend Your Summer Vacation." *INC.,* July 1990.

Lusterman, S. *Trends in Corporate Education and Training, Report #870.* New York: The Conference Board, 1985.

National Academy of Engineering, 2101 Constitution Ave. NW, Washington, DC 20418.

National Society for Performance and Instruction. *Introduction to Performance Technology, Vol. 1.* Washington, DC: 1986.

Nilson, C. *How to Manager Training.* New York: AMACOM, 1991; and 2nd ed., 1998.

____, *Training for Non-Trainers, A Do-It-Yourself Guide for Managers.* New York: AMACOM, 1990.

____, *Training Program Workbook & Kit.* Paramus, NJ: Prentice Hall, 1989.

Reich, R. B. "The Real Economy." *The Atlantic Monthly,* February 1991, pp. 35-51.

Rothwell, William J. *ASTD Models for Human Performance Improvement: Roles, Competencies, and Outputs.* Alexandria, VA: American Society for Training & Development, 1996.

Simpson, E. J. *The Classification of Objectives, Psychomotor Domain.* Urbana, IL: University of Illinois, 1966.

Stamps, David. "Community Colleges Go Corporate" in *Training,* December 1995.

Thomas, R. R. Jr. *Beyond Race and Gender.* New York: AMACOM, 1991.

Thompson, G. L. "Training's Salary Survey 1990." *Training,* November 1990.

Training Magazine Industry Report 1998: An Overview of Employee Training in America. Minneapolis, MN: Lakewood Publications, October 1998.

U.S. Congress, Office of Technology Assessment. *Worker Training: Competing in the New International Economy, OTA-ITE-457.* Washington, DC: U.S. Government Printing Office, September 1990.

U.S. Department of Commerce, National Institute of Standards and Technology. *Malcolm Baldrige National Quality Award, 1991 Application Guidelines.* Gaithersburg, MD: 1990.

____, *1998 Criterion for Performance Excellence,* and *1998 Application Forms and Instructions.* Gaithersburg, MD: 1997.

Carolyn Nilson is a veteran trainer with wide experience in traditional and state-of-the-art training assignments. Among the corporations and agencies she has served as consultant in training design are: American Management Association, Chemical Bank, Chevron, Dun & Bradstreet, Martin-Marietta, and many others.

Nilson was a member of the technical staff at AT&T Bell Laboratories where she was part of the Standards, Audits, and Inspections Group of the Systems Training Center. There she developed, implemented, and promoted quality standards in course design and delivery. She also taught the Bell Labs' train-the-trainer course.

She held the position of manager of simulation training at Combustion Engineering, where she managed the training operation and created high-level computer-based training for international clients. Nilson was also director of training for a systems consulting firm with a broad base of *Fortune* 500 clientele in the New York City metropolitan area. In this position, she supervised a staff of training consultants and was responsible for client training analysis, design, implementation, and evaluation.

She has been a faculty member for Padgett-Thompson seminars, the Ziff Institute, Center for the Study of Work Teams, the U.S. Armed Services Training Institute, and the USAID's Management Development Initiative in Cairo, Egypt. She is an active member of the ASTD, where she was part of a grassroots planning task force in the area of human resource development skills and strategies. She has been an advisor to The MASIE Center in the areas of learning strategies and learning standards.

Nilson received her doctorate in education from Rutgers University with a specialty in measurement and evaluation in vocational and technical education.

She is a noted speaker and the author of numerous magazine articles, training papers, and training manuals. In addition, she has a long list of books to her credit, including many that have been chosen for book clubs, including the Macmillan Executive Book Club, the Newbridge Book Club, Soundview Executive Books Summaries, and the Business Week Book Club. Carolyn Nilson has authored four out of amazon.com's "50 Best Selling Training Books."